Conten

CW00840578

Introduction   1

Note for driving instructors   5

Chapter One: How to use this book   9

Chapter Two: Involve your instructor   25

Chapter Three: What makes a good driver?   29

Chapter Four: Your baseline competence level   35

Chapter Five: Your baseline confidence level   51

Chapter Six: The basics   65

Chapter Seven: Mastering the manoeuvres   87

Chapter Eight: How much is your personality costing you?   101

Chapter Nine: Dyslexic and dyspraxic dilemma   125

Chapter Ten: Toxins—are they influencing your driving?   159

Chapter Eleven: When do you want to pass your test?   167

Chapter Twelve: Are you talking yourself into failure?   173

Chapter Thirteen: Test day stress-busters   183

Chapter Fourteen: The top ten reasons for failure
                            and how to avoid them   201

Chapter Fifteen: You've passed – now what?   217

Further reading and useful contacts   226

L of a way 2 Pass

Diane Hall

authorHOUSE®

AuthorHouse™ UK Ltd.
500 Avebury Boulevard
Central Milton Keynes, MK9 2BE
www.authorhouse.co.uk
Phone: 08001974150

First published by AuthorHouse 11/5/2008
ISBN: 978-1-4389-0958-5 (sc)

Printed in the United States of America
Bloomington, Indiana

This book is printed on acid-free paper.

'Those who say it cannot be done should not interrupt those who are doing it.'

anon.

'Until you believe that you can do it, you can't'.

anon.

L of a way 2 Pass

By

Diane Hall DSA(ADI), TFT-Alg.

Edited by Rebecca Collins, BA(Hons)

With contributions by

Sandra Read, Cert. In Ed., OCR Diploma, SpLD, MPNLP

Sean Quigley, TFT-VT, MPNLP, Cert.E.H.

Acknowledgements

I would like to give my heartfelt thanks to the following people; Sandra Read for her specialist help and advice on dyslexia and dyspraxia, Sean Quigley for his immense knowledge of Thought Field Therapy and how toxins can adversely affect us, Dr. Roger Callahan for Thought Field Therapy which has changed the lives of millions of people, Janet Thomson who kindly allowed me to use her information on 'Specific Reversal', Dr. Candace Pert with her amazing work on 'molecules of emotion', all of my pupils over the last year who have helped me with this project, and Steve Light of Breadandbuddha for website design.

Thanks also to my partner, Dave, who has been so patient whilst I've spent endless hours at the computer, and for thinking of this brilliant title!

Special thanks to Rebecca Collins for her editing skills, and tireless dedication and enthusiasm for this book, making sense of my ideas and presenting them in a legible fashion.

Finally, my warmest thanks to UnLtd for providing a Millennium Awards Trust Grant for Social Entrepreneurs without which this project may still have been just an idea floating around in my head!

Introduction

Every year, over half of the driving tests conducted will result in failure!

Reading the above statement, I'm sure you'll agree that that's an awful lot of very disappointed people. Over the years, I have taught many people to drive, and during this time, I have become increasingly disheartened at the number of really good drivers who fail their test because of nerves on the day.

In addition to this, I was also concerned about the number of repetitive lessons that I was teaching because pupils seemed to be forgetting much of what they had been taught from one lesson to the next.

I believed that pupils were spending more money on repetitive lessons and tests than necessary, so I decided that there had to be a better way for me to help pupils to pass their test, and ultimately become safe, thoughtful and considerate drivers. To this end, I researched different methods that would help pupils to increase their ability and confidence, and enable them to reduce their stress and nerves on test day. The results of this research form the basis of this book.

Used correctly, this book will enable you to reduce the number of lessons and tests that you require. If, as a result of using the techniques in this book, you pass your test in just five less lessons, that's a saving of over £100, not to mention the immense relief that you will feel having been able to take, and pass, your driving test feeling calm, relaxed and in control.

If you want to find out how effective these methods are, check out the testimonials for the methods described in this book at www.tapstherapy.co.uk

Learning to drive -
An exciting or scary prospect for you?

When it comes to learning a new skill, such as driving, people often vary dramatically in their attitude and approach. Frequently, I will be contacted by pupils a few weeks before their seventeenth birthday, because they have obtained their driving licence and want a lesson on their birthday because they can't wait to get started.

Conversely, many people are put off learning to drive because they find the prospect scary and don't want to contemplate having to face such a daunting task.

If you fall into the first category, you are very lucky; when you enjoy something, you tend to be good at it because you are dedicated to succeeding, and this book will go a long way to making sure you have a successful test pass in as short a time as possible.

If you fall into the second category, all is certainly not lost. After reading this book and working through the exercises and techniques, you will find that learning to drive is not such a daunting prospect after all; you may even get to enjoy it!

Throughout the book, you will find successfully proven methods and techniques that work. With the aid of this book, I feel confident that you will be able to increase your driving ability, your self-assurance will soar, and you can eliminate test day nerves.

Now you need to ask yourself; are you ready for that? If you already feel completely confident in your ability, believe that you can perform all the manoeuvres correctly, drive totally without your instructor's help and guidance, and are totally confident in your ability to pass your test, then stop reading this book now and put it back on the shelf because you don't need it.

However, if there is the slightest doubt in your mind about your confidence or competence levels, or you think that 'nerves' will get the better of you on your test, then read on, this book has been written especially for you.

Note for driving instructors

This book is NOT a driving manual, nor is it intended to replace the role of the ADI, but to provide yourself and your pupils with additional methods and techniques that will enable capable drivers to pass their test without nerves getting in the way, and to reduce the number of times that you have to keep repeating the same basic instructions.

As driving instructors we all have the same goal in mind; to get our pupils' driving to a standard required for the test in the least amount of lessons, whilst at the same time making sure that they become safe, confident and considerate drivers. Specific visualisation exercises provided in this book will help focus your pupils' attention on their driving in between lessons. This will help to ensure that they haven't forgotten everything that you taught them previously, thus helping to reduce the repetition during lessons. Other techniques used will increase your pupils' confidence and competence levels, therefore making the learning process much more enjoyable and less frustrating for both yourself and your pupil.

There is also a stress-busting section which aims to reduce test day nerves, therefore ensuring the best possible chance of your pupil passing their test on the first attempt, provided of course that they are at the required standard.

We all have different methods of teaching; ask any instructor how they teach reverse park, and although the result is the same, the method often varies. Therefore, I have intentionally refrained from giving specific instructions as they may conflict with your own method, and only serve to confuse your pupil. If used correctly, this book will greatly assist and speed up the learning process, and therefore it will be helpful for your pupil if you work with them by completing the 'specifics' where necessary, in the spaces provided. Your pupil will then be able to visualise between lessons what you have been teaching them. For example, if you teach a reverse park, ordinarily you may find your pupil has often forgotten how to do it by the next lesson. However, if a pupil is willing to spend just a few minutes a day in between lessons visualising the manoeuvre, then they are much more likely to remember it for the following lesson. This works in much the same way as learning the words to a song; if you just hear it once, you won't remember it, but play it every day and soon enough you will know the words off by heart.

We are all trained to teach the standard syllabus to prepare a pupil for their driving test, however, I believe that the standardised training doesn't go deep enough into the psychology of learning. It was only because of my frustration with this that I decided to investigate further and to put into practice the methods described in this book.

Four percent of the population is diagnosed as dyslexic. It is estimated that at least ten percent of the population may have some form of dyslexia. However, many experts agree that the real figure is likely to be much higher. Therefore, the likelihood is that several of your pupils may be dyslexic. Before I started researching this book, I like many people didn't realise how debilitating dyslexia can be for learner drivers. It's often difficult as instructors to accept that our standard method of teaching is not always the most appropriate for every learner, and your pupils who are dyslexic will benefit from multi-sensory learning techniques to help them to take information on board more easily.

Like many people, I didn't know an awful lot about dyslexia, so therefore I have enlisted the help of an expert on dyslexia. A specialist chapter has been written by Sandra Read to aid all learners who are dyslexic. However, this advice will benefit all of your pupils, regardless of whether your pupil is dyslexic or not. I suggest that you have a look at her techniques for 'multi-sensory learning' as you will find these will enhance your ability to convey information. Before I researched these methods pupils tended to forget so much from one lesson to the next. After putting into practice Sandra's ideas, I found that pupils could remember much more from their previous lessons.

If you take on board Sandra's suggestions in Chapter Nine, 'Dyslexic and dyspraxic dilemma', you are taking the first steps in really helping your dyslexic learners to learn in the manner which they find most suitable. You may not find all the suggestions work for you and your pupils, but experiment and find what does work. I am interested in hearing from instructors who have used these techniques and to what effect, and also any other techniques that you find useful for any group of learners who experience learning difficulties, as these hints and tip can be posted onto the website to benefit other instructors and pupils.

I truly believe that it's time to revamp our ideas as instructors, and to develop a person centred approach to learning, rather than just following the set syllabus. These techniques really do work. Please, try them with your pupils and see the difference for yourself. You will find that with the help of these techniques your pupils will learn easily, enjoy their lessons more, and definitely be less 'stressed out' over their test!

I hope that over time, these techniques will become standard practice, and as instructors we will help to produce confident, competent drivers who are thoughtful, considerate, and above all, safe. However, this can only happen with your help and input. It's very easy to mock something that we are not familiar with, and to be honest I was very sceptical until I started to use these techniques for myself. You know yourself how pupils differ from each other on test day; some are laid back and calm, whereas others are so nervous that they even cry or are physically sick. After using the stress busting techniques, you may find it seems like you are teaching a different pupil!

If you have found this book useful and want to learn more about the techniques used, the relevant websites are at the back of the book, or you can contact me via the book's website at www.Lofaway2pass.com

Chapter One

How to use this book

Firstly, this book is not intended as a driving manual.
It cannot replace your driving lessons; rather it's aim is to complement them.

The intention of this book is to enable you to recall effectively what you have learnt during your driving lessons, without you having to repeat newly taught manoeuvres etc. over and over again in your subsequent lessons. In other words, the book should be used to reinforce skills, not teach them. I wanted to call this book 'How to keep your driving instructor sane and not drive him round the bend'. The reason I chose the eventual title was that this book really does give you the easiest, simplest, most effective way of passing your test stress-free and in fewer lessons than had you not used this book. In essence, it really is a hell of an easy way to pass your driving test.

With exception to Chapter Six, 'The basics', I have intentionally avoided using 'how to drive' instructions, particularly with regard to manoeuvres. These can only be learnt hands-on during driving lessons. My aim is to supplement rather than replace the skills you are learning from your driving instructor.

Therefore, space has been provided for you to note down, with the help of your driving instructor, what you have learnt. This will help reinforce your knowledge. If you take a few minutes each day to complete the exercises you will find that you can remember much more from your previous lesson than you did before and you will find that you are much better prepared for your next lesson.

Do I have to read the whole book?

This book is not meant to be read from cover to cover, unless of course you want to, but rather it's aim is to identify areas where you may need some help. You will then be able to use the relevant sections to improve these areas. I suggest that you start off by reading Chapter Two, 'Involve your instructor' as this will ensure that you get the most benefit from the combined use of this book and your lessons, then read Chapter Three, 'What makes a good driver' as you will learn from this what you are aiming for in order to be the best driver that you can possibly be.

There is a specialist chapter written by Sandra Read to aid all learners who are dyslexic. Sandra has provided some wonderful advice that will benefit anyone learning to drive, regardless if you are dyslexic or not. I suggest that you have a look at her techniques for 'multi-sensory learning' in Chapter Nine, 'Dyslexic and dyspraxic dilemma' as you will find these will speed up the overall learning process resulting in less repetitive lessons, and therefore ultimately passing your test sooner and saving yourself money.
Sean Quigley who is a leading authority on Thought Field Therapy, has given some wonderful advice on how toxins can have an adverse affect on anyone learning to drive. You will find this in Chapter Ten, 'Toxins - are they influencing your driving ability?'

How can this book help me to become a good driver?

I hope that by working through the exercises and techniques relevant to you, you will find your personal confidence growing day by day and as this happens your competence will naturally grow dramatically. I firmly believe that such competence cannot be achieved by driving lessons alone. You will soon find yourself mastering those manoeuvres easily, performing those hill starts perfectly, and tackling roundabouts with total ease.

So, which exercises do I need to do?

Firstly, you will need to assess your baseline confidence and competence levels, so do the exercises in Chapter Four, 'Your baseline competence', and Chapter Five, 'Your baseline confidence', which will help you to determine your particular strengths and weaknesses and this will pinpoint what areas you need help with.

After that, you can dip into the sections of the book most relevant to you. If you are just starting off, or wish to check your basic skills level, I recommend you do the exercises in Chapter Six, 'The basics', or if you are struggling with manoeuvres, you can dip into Chapter Seven, 'Master the manoeuvres'. Quite often our own personality can hinder our progress. I encourage you to take a quick look at Chapter Eight, 'How much is your personality costing you?' Did you know that what you think affects how you drive? Do you often say to your instructor: 'I hate hill starts, I **always** stall!'? If this is the case, then have a look at Chapter Twelve, 'Are you talking yourself into failure?'

Many of the exercises and techniques are beneficial for several areas with which you may have an issue. For example, you may feel a great deal of frustration because you can't get a manoeuvre correct, and a similar feeling of frustration if you have previously failed a driving test. The same technique to eliminate your feeling of frustration can be used for both of these situations. Therefore, you may find an exercise repeated with a slightly different aspect to it in different chapters. For the exercises using Thought Field Therapy, you will find comprehensive instructions at the end of this chapter for using this fantastic technique.

Finally, you've reached it—your driving test!

Of course, the reason that you bought this book is to enable you to pass your driving test easily and become a good driver. I suggest you **don't** skip Chapter Fourteen, 'The top ten reasons for failure and how to avoid them' as reading this may mean the difference between a pass or a fail.

How can I prove to the examiner that I am a good driver?

When you have increased your competence and confidence levels, mastered the manoeuvres, and become a good driver, the next step is passing your driving test. Although you may now feel that you are physically capable of passing your test, how do you feel about it? In a recent survey* sixty-five percent of pupils said that they felt really nervous about their test and that they thought that they would fail due to 'doing something silly'. The driving test is based on your ability to drive to a certain standard, and even though the examiner will appreciate that you are nervous, this won't help you if you make a serious mistake, because the examiner needs to be sure that you can drive competently under such circumstances.

The aim of this book is to help eliminate the apprehension you would normally feel in a driving test. All too often I've seen a really good driver fail their test due to nerves getting the better of them. Therefore, there is a whole section dedicated to eliminating test day nerves, giving you the best chance possible of passing your test stress-free on your first attempt, providing of course that you are capable of driving to the required standard.

Imagine how it would feel to totally wipe out stress, be prepared for your test, and pass with confidence. You owe it to yourself to do everything you can to pass your test first time. I suggest that Chapter Thirteen, 'Test day stress-busters' is essential reading.

Changing tests

At the time of writing, Driving Standards Agency are in the process of looking at amending the driving test so that it reflects more accurately driving on the roads of today. At present, this is under consultation, and it will perhaps be many months or even longer before a new test is introduced. However, even if the test is substantially altered, it does not alter anything that you will learn in this book as the aim is to make you a safe, confident and competent driver, no matter how Driving Standards Agency decide to test you.

Your driving instructor will advise you of any proposed changes to the driving test, but I would suggest that you also check the book's website: www.Lofaway2pass.com as I will be updating that on a regular basis with news and comments that are of interest. You can also log onto the blog for the book.

Techniques to help you

This section will give you a brief overview of what techniques you will be using in the various exercises throughout this book, and how to use them. These techniques have been proven effective over decades and have been used by many successful people to achieve their goals. You now have the opportunity to put these methods to the test yourself and benefit as millions of other people around the world have done.

Thought Field Therapy
TFT

Thought Field Therapy (TFT) was developed by Roger Callahan and is a natural, drug-free therapy which is brief and effective in treating all manner of issues, including emotional stress, trauma, anxiety, phobias and a range of other afflictions that may hinder you. As a qualified Thought Field Therapist, I am using TFT techniques in this book to help with a range of issues, including eliminating test day nerves, increasing your ability to visualise yourself performing the manoeuvres perfectly, taking away any negative emotions left over from previous tests, leaving you with a clean slate to take your test with no emotional baggage, and the ability to take away anger, frustration etc. Thought Field Therapy has been helping millions of people over decades and has a very high success rate.

TFT utilises acupressure points, which you activate by simply tapping them with your fingertips whilst thinking about the specific issue that you want to resolve. This process has the capability of disabling and often completely eliminating the issue that you are thinking of, whether it be the fear of taking the test, or performing a manoeuvre that you find difficult.

I believe that TFT is the most effective psychotherapy. Time after time, it has proven to be extremely effective in treating a range of issues including fears, anxiety, phobias, trauma, and helping you to visualise yourself performing at the peak of your ability.

The good thing about TFT is that you don't have to believe in it for it to work. Antibiotics don't depend upon you believing in them for them to work, and it's the same for TFT. If you follow the guidelines, you will find it works whether you feel completely confident in it or are sceptical about it.

Neuro Linguistic Programming
NLP

NLP is a set of behaviours, skills and attitudes that help us to understand how we organise information and communicate with others. It enables us to know what is useful to others in ways that allow them to achieve beyond what they could previously conceive; in this case, enabling you to visualise performing at your peak and passing your test easily.

NLP has been used by successful people in all walks of life to achieve their goals. It is one of the systems used by Paul McKenna to enable him to help people overcome fears and phobias or develop a more positive attitude to challenges in their lives. Put very simply, it is a form of 'brain training'.

Broken down into its component parts Neuro Linguistic Programming means:

Neuro
The nervous system, through which experience is received and processed through the five senses.

Linguistic
Language and nonverbal communication systems through which neural representations are coded, ordered and given meaning.

Programming
The ability to organise our communication and neurological systems to achieve specific desired results and goals.

Although the description of NLP seems a little confusing, don't worry as the exercises themselves are very simple and easy to perform. NLP and TFT are the principle techniques that you will be using to enable you to pass your driving test stress free and in fewer lessons. Each of these techniques is multi-faceted, i.e. it has many different applications, and you will gain the full benefit of them throughout this book.

Using Thought Field Therapy

As I stated above, TFT is extremely effective and you will find that the issues that you want to resolve will be easily achieved using TFT. There are different acupressure points on your body, and tapping each of these has a different effect. Therefore, it's important to get the best results that you tap the correct points in the correct order. Rather like cooking, you have to have the basic ingredients and use them in the correct order otherwise the result is not very good!

There is a standard procedure to follow, but you will find that there are different **Basic Tapping Sequences**, depending on the issue that you want to resolve. Throughout the book, there are suggestions of what TFT exercises are going to be of benefit to you. Rather than repeating the exercise in each chapter, you just need to refer back to this chapter for the **Basic Tapping Sequence** for the issue that you are dealing with, then follow the procedure as described further on in this chapter.

You will be asked to tap several of the following places on your body, and in differing orders. These sequences have been formulated over many years and have been found to be the most effective; therefore, it's important that you follow them accurately. When asked to do so, you tap each point about five times with two fingers.

Eyebrow: At the beginning of the eyebrow, just above the bridge of nose.

Outside of Eye: At the outside edge of eyebrow.

Under Eye: About 2cm below the bottom of the eyeball, at the bottom centre of the bony part, high on the cheek.

Collarbone: About 2cm down and to the left or right of where you would knot a tie.

Under Arm: About 10cm directly below the armpit on the ribs.

Tiny Finger: Inside tip of the tiny finger, adjacent to the nail, and on the side closest to the thumb.

Middle Finger: Inside tip of the middle finger, adjacent to the nail, and on the side closest to the thumb.

Index Finger: Inside tip of the index finger, adjacent to the nail, and on the side closest to the thumb.

Under Nose: Under your nose, above the top lip.

Outside of Hand: Outside edge of the hand, about midway between the wrist and the base of the little finger, the part of the hand that you would use for a karate chop.

Gamut Spot: On the back of the hand about 2cm below the raised knuckles of the ring finger and little finger when making a fist.

Now you are familiar with the tapping points, below is listed the **Basic Tapping Sequence** that you need to use for each issue. Remember, some of the actions that you are asked to perform may seem a little odd, but it's important that you follow them accurately, as they have been discovered after many years of clinical research and each are relevant. As I mentioned earlier, different tapping points have different effects, therefore when you see

Basic Tapping Sequence, you need to use the sequence described for the issue that you are dealing with. It's no good using the basic tapping sequence for fear when you want to eliminate frustration, and vice versa.

When you come to an exercise in a particular chapter, you will be told which Basic Tapping Sequence you need to use for the particular issue; you can then refer to this chapter, and find the correct sequence. The following is a list of these sequences.

Basic Tapping Sequences

Eliminating past trauma or upset
Eyebrow, Under Eye, Under Arm, Collarbone

Anxiety, nerves, stress, or issues such as hill starts, manoeuvres etc. which may cause you to panic
Under Eye, Under Arm, Collarbone

Visualisation for peak performance
Under Arm, Collarbone

Intimidation for challenging circumstances, such as feeling intimidated by the examiner
Eyebrow, Under Eye, Under Nose, Collarbone, Tiny Finger

Guilt, such as feeling that you have let people down if you have failed
Index Finger, Collarbone

Anger
Tiny Finger, Collarbone

Frustration and impatience
Eyebrow, Under Eye, Under Arm, Collarbone, Tiny Finger, Collarbone

Alternative for frustration**
Tiny Finger, Middle Finger

Severe frustration**
Outside of Eye, Tiny Finger, Middle Finger

Abuse**
Index Finger, Outside of Eye

Embarrassment
Under Nose

Enhancement of motivation
Under Eye, Collarbone, Under Eye

Increasing your self-esteem
Eyebrow, Under Eye, Under Arm, Collarbone, Under Nose, Chin, Collarbone, Middle Finger

When I first tried Thought Field Therapy, I thought the process would be hard to learn and quite lengthy. You will find that you have to read through the process a few times before it sinks in, and it doesn't matter if you read it whilst doing the exercise: you don't have to memorise it. However, you will find that after a few times of using these techniques they will become quite natural to you. Please don't be tempted to skip any of it; remember that doing these exercises will help you to pass your test stress free in fewer lessons. Ask yourself this; is it worth a little time spent now to save you a lot of time and money?

Your Personal Treatment Sequence

1. Think of the issue and work up as much discomfort as you can. In your mind, rate your discomfort on a scale of 1 to 10 with a score of 10 being the highest degree of discomfort. Do not spend more than a few moments on this phase. When you feel that your anxiety (or the problem you are working on) is at a peak, begin Step 2.

2. Go through your tapping sequence; using two finger tips, tap solidly about five times on each of the treatment points in the Basic Tapping Sequence recommended for the issue that you are working on.

3. Re-evaluate the issue on the 1 to 10 scale again. If the intensity of emotional discomfort has decreased by 2 points or more, go to Step 4. If it has not gone down by 2 points or more then follow this procedure; tap the side of either hand where you would do a karate chop. Repeat Step 2 (your tapping sequence) before going onto Step 4.

4. Keep your head still, and tap the 'gamut spot' whilst doing the following:
Close your eyes
Open your eyes
Look down and to the right, eyes back to centre
Look down and to the left, eyes back to centre
Roll your eyes in a circle one way and then in the opposite direction
Hum a few notes of any tune
Count to five
Hum a few notes of any tune

continued...

5. Re-evaluate the level of your emotional discomfort. If your emotional discomfort has reduced to a 0 or 1, go to Step 6. If it is not down to 0 or 1, repeat Step 2, your Basic Tapping Sequence then Step 4, then Step 2 again.   Keep repeating this procedure until your emotional discomfort is at 0 or 1, then finally move onto Step 6.

6. Floor to ceiling eye roll. If your emotional discomfort level is much lower, but not completely gone, you need to begin tapping the gamut spot. Hold your head facing forward and still. Now, without moving your head, use your eyes to look down toward the floor and then, gradually, to the count of 6 or 7, vertically raise your eyes until looking at the ceiling, all the while tapping the gamut spot.

Staying out of 'Psychological Reversal'

Psychological Reversal (PR) is an extremely important factor in Thought Field Therapy. It can block the effects of an otherwise successful therapy and can cause people to become self-defeating and negativistic. Self-sabotage is the result. When you are Psychologically Reversed, your actions and feelings can run contrary to what you want to do and how you want to feel. As PR can affect you in many different ways, you will find out how to test yourself for PR and how to deal with the different aspects of it in several chapters.

> **It is essential to keep yourself out of
> Psychological Reversal.
> The correction for PR is simple.
> Tap the side of your hand where you would
> perform a karate chop 10 or so times.
> Do this several times every day to ensure that you stay
> 'positive'.**

Many people who are dyslexic are Psychologically Reversed and if you are dyslexic, I would suggest that you perform the correction several times a day in order to ensure that you stay out of Psychological Reversal.

I find that many of my pupils get their lefts and rights muddled up; this is usually a classic sign of PR. It is very easy to correct; just perform the correction as described above and you should find you can easily remember your left from your right. Let's face it, this is very important when learning to drive and also when trying to follow directions.

*Survey conducted by the author on fifty pupils at various stages of driving.
** My thanks to Sean Quigley for these sequences.

Chapter Two

Involve your instructor

As you have read previously, this book is intended to complement not replace your driving lessons, and it will be most effective if you use it in conjunction with your driving lessons. I suggest that you explain to your instructor that you are using this book to help you to learn more easily and effectively, so that you can benefit more from each lesson that you take. Most of the exercises are designed to be done anytime, but for some, it's helpful to perform them on your lesson, to reinforce your instructor's teaching.

For example, if you are learning a new manoeuvre, then the visualisation exercise in Chapter Seven, 'Mastering the manoeuvres' is much more effective if you take a few minutes to do the exercise on your lesson whilst it is fresh in your mind. Your instructor may say that this will take time from your lesson; however, I assure you, a few minutes taken doing the exercise on your lesson will save you and your instructor a lot of time in subsequent lessons as you will find you remember how to do the manoeuvre more easily and your instructor will not have to keep repeating how to do it.

Stuck in our ways!

If you are lucky enough to have a good instructor, they are likely to be open to trying any techniques that will help you, as their objective is to get you through your test and train you to become a safe, competent driver. However, if your instructor is not keen on working with you with these techniques and letting you try them during your lesson, then you should ask yourself if they really do have your best interests at heart.

People are often 'stuck in their ways', and driving instructors are certainly no exception to this. I know if a pupil said to me 'my friend says his instructor does it like this...', then a natural reaction would be to feel undermined and to go on the defensive about my own method. Therefore, if you are happy with how your instructor is teaching you, it's very important to tell them this, and explain that that you are using this book to enhance your driving lessons with them, and that you are more than happy with your lessons.

If someone else had written this book before me and a pupil had brought it along with them on their driving lesson, my first thought might have been 'it's probably a load of rubbish!' However, if I had felt that the pupil may benefit from it, I would at least have given it a try. You may well find that your instructor has a similar attitude. We all tend to think that our way is best, and can feel insulted if we feel that we're being asked to try something different. Ask your instructor to have an open mind, and use which exercises and techniques work for you both. The best approach to any learning is to be flexible, and use what suits you. There's no point in using something that you don't feel comfortable with.

If your instructor is amenable to trying the different methods and techniques in this book with you, then you should both find that the learning process is made much more enjoyable and certainly less frustrating for both of you.

However, if your instructor is adamant that this book won't help you, and that they don't want to be involved with any of the methods, but you don't want to change your instructor, I suggest that you learn as much as you can from each lesson, and then use this book between lessons to enhance what you learned on your lesson. If your instructor is pleased with your progress, perhaps you can tell them that you have been using the book between lessons; they may then be more willing to give it a try!

Chapter Three

What makes a good driver?

Before I was a driving instructor, I was a riding instructor. It used to amaze me how much people differed in the varying amounts of time and effort they needed to acquire the skills necessary for riding a horse. A person could get on a horse for the first time in their life and look like they were born in the saddle, whereas another person could have lesson after lesson and still not look at all comfortable in the saddle.

When I first trained to be a driving instructor, I should have realised how people's ability could vary, but I naively believed that I would teach a standard syllabus and that if I taught consistently, then pupils would learn at the same rate, and would therefore be ready for their test after a set number of lessons. How wrong I was.

If we were all the same, everyone would have a brain like Einstein, play football like Wayne Rooney, and be able to sing like Pavarotti!

As someone anonymously once said: 'In a hundred people, one finds all kinds'. However, that's not much good to you if you need to learn to drive and don't feel that you have a natural talent for it, or if you are simply not progressing as quickly as you would like or expect to.

Over the years I have taught many pupils of varying abilities, ranging from one extreme to another; from a lady who was very frustrated because she had spent about £3000 on 150 hours of lessons with several different instructors, to a pupil who passed his test on his tenth hour, and even then wasn't happy as he got one minor driving fault on his test sheet.

After getting frustrated with this I decided to try to find out why some pupils were capable of passing their driving test much sooner than others even though they had been taught in exactly the same way. Over a period of time, I noted the number of lessons different pupils required in order to be successful on their test. During my research I considered age, gender, height, ethnicity, social background, academic intelligence and a range of other factors. I discovered that:

**Every good driver possess, above all else,
equal amounts of confidence and competence**

All the other factors that I considered appeared to be largely irrelevant. I came to believe that if the pupil's confidence and competence levels were evenly matched, then they stood the greatest chance of passing their driving test stress-free on their first attempt and with the least amount of lessons possible, and becoming a safe, thoughtful and considerate driver.

What happens when your competence and confidence levels aren't matched?

If you have a high skill level, but aren't very confident, then it will take you longer to pass your test because you will not have enough faith in your own ability. Ultimately, you are likely to become a safe, considerate driver, but getting to this stage will take longer than necessary, and at high expense in terms of time and money. If however, you are a very confident person, but don't have the skill level to back this up, then your confidence is misplaced, and you run a serious risk of trying to take your test too soon with the possibility of being a danger on the road.

How many fatal accidents are caused by drivers being over-confident in their ability?

Whilst it is undoubtedly true that many accidents are caused by over confidence, it may also be argued that a lack of confidence resulting in hesitancy, failure to keep up with the rest of the traffic and general nervous driving can also be a danger to a certain extent.

The following graph shows what happens when your competence and confidence levels vary. When you have equal amounts of both, then you are at your optimum point; you are the best that you can be. You will find that as your confidence increases, so does your competence, and vice versa. There is no 'upper limit' to competence; we all learn from experience. However, the more over-confident you become, the more your competence decreases because you will believe that you are more capable than you actually are.

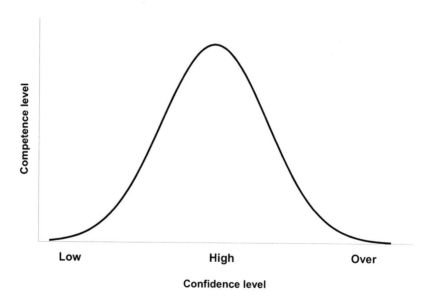

In order to be the best driver that you can be you need to aim for equal competence and confidence when driving, and if either one is lacking, to boost it to the optimum level. Therefore, you need to do the exercises in the next two chapters to determine your baseline levels. These will enable you to pinpoint your trouble spots and fix them quickly.

I'm doing it because you told me to!

I consider a good driver to be someone who thinks for themselves, and acts appropriately on what they see with due care and consideration for other road users. In a nutshell, good drivers use **common sense**. This may sound very strange as you would assume that everyone uses their common sense when it comes to driving. However, in my experience, this is not always the case. When it comes to driving, common sense is not always something that comes naturally to everyone; however with the help of this book, you will find that your common sense increases in line with your competence and confidence.

So often a learner will do something because I have told them to, and it's the 'rule'; for example, the Mirror Signal Manoeuvre routine is often carried out by a pupil because that's what the instructor has told them to do, and not because it's the logical thing to do. The faster a pupil is able to move away from doing something because their instructor told them to, to doing it because it's the sensible thing to do, the faster they are going to learn to drive, pass their test, and become a safe, considerate driver.

Taking responsibility for your actions

Rules and laws are obviously necessary for all sorts of things, including learning to drive. It's the law that you stop at a red light and go on green if it's safe to do so. If we didn't have this rule, then everything would erupt in chaos. The good driver however, is the one that understands the principles behind the rules, and acts appropriately. It's crucially important that as a driver, you take responsibility for your own actions.

Chapter Four

Your baseline competence level

Natural born talent is an often-used phrase to describe someone who can just pick up a skill with seeming ease. We all know of great sportsmen and women, singers, artists and scientists who appear to have 'natural born talent', but have you ever wondered why these particular people are at the top of their chosen profession? What sets apart David Beckham and Wayne Rooney from someone who plays in the Sunday League? There is of course the great nature/nurture debate, i.e. are we born with natural talent, or is it learned? Whichever plays the most important role, nature or nurture, the following is definitely true;

these people only made it to the top of their chosen profession with huge amounts of drive, enthusiasm and the dedication to succeed.

Whilst I'm not suggesting that in order to learn to drive you need the total 24/7 dedication and commitment that these people exhibit, the more time and effort you decide to commit to learning to drive will certainly pay off. By reading this book, you are taking the first step to accelerating the learning process by working on your competence and confidence levels between your driving lessons.

A person at the top of their profession may have natural talent, but it's how they ultimately develop their talent that makes the difference and puts them at the top. A top athlete maybe able to run faster, jump higher or score more goals than the competition, but they won't be able to keep doing so without lots of hard work and dedication as well.

It stands to reason that everyone has differing abilities; that top athlete probably has a useless singing voice, or that successful racing driver has the artistic ability of an average ten year old.

For every skill, each person's 'core competence level' differs, and this of course includes learning to drive

This is why some people seem naturally able to pass their test much sooner than others, and quickly become good drivers. Perhaps you can recall a time when you have been a passenger and felt really safe, as the driver had a very smooth, relaxing and confident drive. However, with some drivers, you may feel that they aren't totally in control and you feel nervous being a passenger.

It's true that we enjoy doing the things that we are good at and shy away from the things that we find difficult. Think of a time when you have tried something new. If you found it difficult, you probably did not enjoy doing it. Every time I teach a pupil who has a natural affinity for driving, they thoroughly enjoy their lessons, progress quickly and easily and relish any new challenge with which I present them. When a pupil struggles with driving, generally they find challenges difficult, and above all do not really look forward to their lessons as they feel that learning to drive is a necessity rather than a pleasurable experience. If you do feel this way, then all is not lost as you will find lots of help and advice in this book that will turn learning to drive from something to endure, to the enjoyable experience that it should be.

What can you do if you don't think that you are a 'natural' driver?

So where does this leave you if you find driving difficult, and realise that it doesn't come naturally to you? Will you instead just travel by bus and taxi, and try to cadge lifts for the rest of your life? I am sure your answer is 'of course not.' Instead you will persevere, with gritted teeth until you finally, with sweaty palms, clutch that elusive pass certificate. You may find that even having passed your test and learnt the skill of driving to the required standard, you still don't feel confident and the thought of having to park between other cars at the supermarket or go on the motorway fills you with dread.

As a driving instructor, in addition to teaching people to drive from the beginning. I also teach 'refresher lessons' to people who have passed their test a long time ago but need help to build their confidence to go on the motorway, park their car, tackle roundabouts etc. They have the physical ability to do these things, but lack the confidence. I know people who have been driving for years, but still plan their routes carefully to avoid certain roads. It doesn't have to be this way.

Picture yourself chatting to friends and telling them that you are really enjoying learning to drive, that you can't wait for your next lesson, and that your instructor said you were one of his best pupils. That would feel better than wishing you were going to the dentist to have a tooth extracted rather than having a driving lesson, wouldn't it? This may come across as extreme, and the likelihood is that the majority of you won't feel this strongly about learning to drive. However, this book is intended to help people of all levels not just the sort of people described above. Whether you are totally new to driving and look on it with a mixture of trepidation and excitement, or you are already well on your way but could do with a boost, you will gain a great deal from working through the various exercises and techniques in this book.

By the end of the book, I believe that you will have greatly increased your natural competence level, and you will find that you will easily be able to deal with any new challenges that your instructor sets you, the number of mistakes you make will reduce rapidly and the enjoyment of learning to drive will increase dramatically.

What is your natural ability and can you increase it?

Two questions will probably be forming in your mind right now: 'How do I rate my own natural ability', and more importantly, 'If it's not very high, what can I do to increase it?' Firstly, we need to look at what abilities and skills you already possess which can help you to become a good driver, and after that you can complete the exercise to assess your current level of ability. There is no absolute rule on how to judge someone's natural ability; it's more of a 'feel', rather like that described in the movie *Dirty Dancing!* You will find that you may already possess certain skills that will be useful when learning to drive. If you have ever ridden a bike, been go-karting, skiing or been on a quad bike etc., then you already have many of the key basic skills that are required for becoming a good driver. The same goes for reading music and playing a musical instrument, or spending endless hours on a play station. Alternatively, consider sports that you enjoy now or have done in the past.

All of these sorts of activities require some degree of hand/eye/foot co-ordination, quick reactions and the ability to assess situations and plan ahead. In addition, it's worth thinking about how you naturally act when you are a passenger in a car. Whenever I drive a pupil back from their driving test, a natural driver will automatically scan the road at every junction to see if it's clear to go, as if they were the driver, even though an Approved Driving Instructor is driving them. However, many pupils would not even consider checking around them if someone else was driving, as the thought would not even enter their head.

Common sense, or not?

I have taught many people to drive, but I am still amazed at the difference between pupils. From very early on, some pupils act without thinking, because to them they are using their 'common sense'. Do the following exercise to find out if you are a 'natural' driver or not.

Are you a 'natural' driver?

Read the following statements and ask yourself whether you do some or all naturally, or only after having been prompted by your instructor. Bear in mind that there is no right or wrong answer; this is just a way of assessing tendencies to behave in one way as opposed to another.

- **Cancelling a signal when necessary, or re-applying if it switches off.**

- **Adjusting your seat and mirrors as soon as you get into the car, and checking that the handbrake is on and the car is in neutral.**

- **Checking your mirrors frequently, because you want to know what's happening around you.**

- **Checking your blind spots.**

- **Scanning junctions on approach rather than waiting until you get to the junction.**

- **Knowing which way to steer whilst reversing without having to think about it.**

- **Changing gear without having to look at the gearlever.**

---

continued...

- Exercising natural awareness and planning; for example, seeing the brake lights of the car in front, and reducing your own speed to maintain a safe distance.

- Remembering to change into first gear when moving off.

- Slowing down when approaching pedestrial crossings.

-Judging distances from cyclists, parked cars etc.

- Even though traffic light is on green, checking both directions just in case emergency vehicle etc. is emerging.

If you feel that any of the above actions come naturally to you, and you do them automatically without your instructor's prompting, then you are lucky as this means that you already possess a good basic skill level for driving. However, don't panic if you can only do all of the above when constantly prompted by your instructor, as by the end of the book, I'm sure you will consider yourself a 'natural driver'!

Why aren't you progressing as quickly as you would like?

After you have had your lesson, you probably won't spend much time thinking about it until the next lesson the following week. If this is the case, then you will have had a whole week to forget what you have been taught, and you will find that during your next lesson your instructor will just be repeating the same thing, and again during the next lesson and the one after that. A pupil who came to me after about six months of learning to drive commented that she didn't feel that she had had 20 lessons, but one lesson repeated 20 times, because she kept forgetting things from one lesson to the next, so therefore in her mind each lesson just seemed to be a repetition of the last one.

Are you prepared to spare five-ten minutes each day improving your driving?

If you are prepared to spend a few minutes each day working through the exercises in this book, then you will find that your driving will become more natural. You will benefit so much more from each lesson and you will be capable of progressing much more quickly than you currently believe possible. Whether you think your current competence level is low or high, by completing the exercises and techniques you will give it a boost. This doesn't mean that you will have to ride a bike, learn to play an instrument or spend hours on a play station before your next driving lesson, but it does require some commitment on your part.

Ask yourself if you are willing to put aside about five-ten minutes a day? If so, by your next lesson, you should find that your competence level will have increased. If however you feel that five-ten minutes a day is too much to commit to, you should really question how much you really want to pass your test with fewer lessons and become a good driver.

Measuring your progress

In order to know that you are benefiting from your driving lessons and this book, you need to have some way of measuring your progress. Many instructors have a progress chart detailing the level you are currently at and how much help you require. Driving Standards Agency also produces their own version, which some instructors use. This is a good method for checking on your progress and making sure that you are learning in a consistent manner. Therefore, I would suggest that you work with whatever method your own instructor uses.

There is a standardised process of learning and you can apply the following method to whatever you are working on with your instructor. I've used learning to ride a bike as an example, as this is something that most people have done. The terms printed in bold may sound baffling, so please refer to the more 'user friendly' explanations that follow:

Unconscious incompetence: you don't know whether you can ride a bike because you haven't tried to yet.

Conscious incompetence: you know you can't ride a bike, because you tried and fell off!

Conscious competence: you can ride a bike, but you have to concentrate on how to do it.

Unconscious competence: you can ride a bike without having to think about how to do it.

If you use this formula to assess your current driving ability, you will find everything you do will fit into one of the above categories. Your instructor will probably have much more meaningful headings such as: 'introduced', 'under instruction', 'prompted', 'seldom prompted', 'independent', 'test standard' or similar. It all amounts to the same thing; assessing whether or not you can do something and labelling to what degree you can do it on your own.

You could probably be 'physically' capable of passing your test after just a few lessons.

People often assume that the physical ability of learning to drive is difficult, and once you have mastered that, the rest is easy. I believe that learning to drive is relatively easy, but the hardest part is being able to do it on your own without your instructor's help. Many people are physically capable of passing their driving test quite soon after starting their lessons; they can look in their mirrors, control the clutch, steer, change gear etc., and that's about all the physical ability that's required. As long as their instructor tells them when to look in their mirrors, when to signal, which lane to be in, whether it's safe to go or not, they could then physically pass their test!

The most difficult aspect of learning to drive is mental, not physical ability.

The knowledge of when to carry out certain actions is not easy to learn, and therefore takes the longest amount of time. If you are already taking lessons, ask yourself how often has your instructor had to repeat seemingly simple instructions, e.g. 'check your mirrors, put your signal on/ take your signal off, remember to take your handbrake off, slower off the clutch?' All of these things should be relatively simple to remember, but an instructor's work is spent repeating these same basic instructions hour after hour! Consider how much faster could you learn to drive if your instructor was able to progress your lessons more quickly because he or she didn't have to keep repeating the same, simple things?

The exercise at the end of this chapter is designed to assess your current competence level. If you have not started driving yet, then you can come back to this exercise after a few lessons to judge your progress. The idea is to get an accurate assessment of everything that you are currently doing on your lessons. I prefer to use the following progress levels: 'introduced', 'prompted', 'seldom prompted', and 'test standard', but feel free to use whichever method you and your instructor prefer. Below is an example of how to complete this exercise. The example used here is turning left and right from a main road into a side road. I would assess a pupil as follows:

Introduced: I will talk a pupil through the whole procedure, from which mirrors to use, when to signal, where to position the car, when to brake, and whether it's safe to go or not.

Prompted: the pupil can carry out the correct procedure, but will probably require some guidance, i.e. prompting to remember to check the appropriate mirrors before signalling or braking, where to position the car, or help with judging when it's safe to go.

Seldom prompted: the pupil is able to carry out left and right turns without help, but will require the occasional prompting because they may have forgotten something, or have not followed the correct order; perhaps for example, slowing down and changing gear before mirror checks and signalling.

Independent/test standard: the pupil only requires directions and is able to safely negotiate the junction with no help or guidance from me, carrying out the procedure in the correct order and choosing the correct lane, appropriate gear and judging when it is safe to go.

I have always found that pupils move easily from under instruction through to seldom prompted, but it's the final push to test standard, the ability to do everything on their own, that is the most difficult. Do the following exercise to establish your current competence level.

Your current competence level

If your instructor already completes a progress chart during your lessons, ask them if you can have a copy of it so you know what your current competence level is for each area that you have been working on.

If your instructor does not complete a progress chart, ask them if they would be prepared to do so because you need a way of judging your progress. If your instructor will not do this, then you can do one on your own, however, it is best if your instructor does do it as they will have a more accurate idea of your ability.

The aim is to know your current capabilities, so you need to think back to what you did on your last lesson, and make a note of how much your instructor needed to help and guide you. You can use the headings that I suggested above if you wish.

It's important that you have an accurate idea of your current ability as it will pinpoint areas that you excel at and also the areas that you require more help with. Once you have completed this, you can use the relevant chapters in the book to help you.

You need to update your chart on a regular basis because this will give you an idea of your progress and again if you are not progressing as quickly as you or your instructor would expect in a particular area, you can discuss with your instructor what you can do during your lessons to combat this, and again use the relevant chapters in the book.

You may find that you disagree with your driving instructor's assessment of your ability. If you believe that you are ready for your test, but your instructor says that you require more lessons, just think back to your last lesson and ask yourself how much your instructor had to prompt you as described above. The most frequently asked question is: 'When can I take my test?' Driving Standard Agency has a very simple reply to this question: 'If you can't do everything without your instructor's help, then you are not ready to take your test.'

By now, you should now have a clear picture of your personal core competence level, where you are with your lessons, and what you need to work on to get you to test standard. After working through the next chapter, you will know if your core competence and confidence levels are equal, or if one needs more of a boost.

Pupil/Instructor notes
You may find that your instructor keeps a note of your progress, but you can use this space for any additional comments that you or your instructor think will be beneficial.

Pupil/Instructor notes

Pupil/Instructor notes

Pupil/Instructor notes

Chapter Five

Your baseline confidence level

Have you ever noticed how some people seem to exude confidence? Are you like this yourself, or do you envy people that seem to have so much confidence in themselves? Even if you feel supremely confident in your driving ability, read this chapter to make sure that you are not over-confident, because where driving is concerned, being overly confident can be more dangerous than a lack of confidence.

Are you born with confidence, or do you develop it?

Some people do appear to have a 'natural' confidence about their personality, but confidence comes from inside, and as we are born neither 'negative' nor 'positive', confidence can be learned, just like any other skill. Throughout this book, you will find many methods and techniques that are specifically designed to increase confidence levels, and all of the exercises that are designed to increase your competence will also be beneficial, as an increase in competence is also going to increase your overall confidence.

Lack of confidence can be a huge problem in life, not just where driving is concerned. This book is primarily designed to increase your confidence and driving ability in order for you to be able to pass your test without stress in fewer lessons, but you may find that by the end of the book, your overall confidence levels have also increased.

Your current confidence levels

Do this quick exercise to assess your current standpoint. Please read the following statement aloud, and make a mental note of your immediate reaction:

'I can't wait to pass my driving test stress-free, and on my first attempt'

How you react to this statement tells you a lot about yourself. What was your first thought when you read this statement?

'No chance, I'll never pass my test first time, and stress-free is a joke; I'll be a bundle of nerves.'

Or

'Of course I will pass my test first time!'

If the former was your immediate reaction, then you are setting yourself up for failure. This is known as a 'self-fulfilling prophecy', and can be either your greatest asset, or your road to failure; the choice is yours. Chapter Twelve, 'Are you talking yourself into failure?' discusses self-fulfilling prophecies in more detail and how they can help you to pass your test stress-free and in fewer lessons.

Do confidence and competence go 'hand in hand'?

An assumption would be that competence and confidence always go hand in hand, and that you can't have one without the other. This is not true. A new pupil may get into my car full of confidence, and as an instructor I may think, 'I've got a good one here', and surprisingly I am not always right, and they are not necessarily as good as I had expected them to be. Alternatively, I may have a pupil who, on their first driving lesson, appears to be really nervous and lacking in confidence. However, they then later may totally surprise themselves, and me, by driving much better than they thought that they would.

Undoubtedly, once your driving ability has increased, you will start to believe in yourself more. However, irrespective of your baseline competence (discussed in the last chapter), wouldn't it be nice to feel confident to start with? In order to stand the best chance of becoming a good driver, you need to have equal confidence and competence. After you have read these first two chapters, you will have a good idea of your baseline levels. You can then decide which chapters are most relevant to you, and work through the various exercises.

So, just how confident are you?

I'm talking generally, and not specifically related to driving. Whether or not you consider yourself a confident person, take a few minutes to complete the following exercise truthfully. You may wish to answer these questions again after you have used the relevant exercises in the book to see how much your confidence has grown.

1. Do I often talk to myself in a 'negative' way, such as telling myself that I am no good at something?

2. When presented with a new challenge, do I worry that I won't be able to do it very well?

3. Do I worry what people think about me?

4. Do I sometimes feel that I have to 'pretend' to be someone that I'm not to impress people, or to get people to like me?

5. When I go for a promotion at work/job interview/ examination etc., does it worry me that I'm not qualified/ prepared/good enough etc.?

6. Do I often feel that I have to 'prove' myself to other people?

7. Do I often picture things that have gone badly previously and keep focusing on them? For example, thinking of a failed driving test or interview.

8. Do I mentally 'beat myself up' for past mistakes?
If your most frequent answer to the above was 'yes', then unfortunately your lack of confidence will not let you progress as quickly as your ability levels would allow because you won't have the belief in yourself to perform to the best of your ability.

So, are you prepared to change?

Although this book is aimed specifically at increasing your confidence with regards to learning to drive, I hope that it will also help to improve your confidence levels generally. Therefore, it is useful for you to know if you are lacking in confidence generally, or to know if your issue is related to learning to drive in particular. It may be that you are in your 'comfort zone' and too scared to try to improve, or perhaps you have achieved great academic, professional or personal success and the only thing you feel a 'failure' at is learning to drive. As you learned in Chapter One, 'How to use this book', this is quite common as people are frequently Psychologically Reversed; it is also possible to be Psychologically Reversed in one specific area or thought. This means that even though you want to be a confident driver, psychologically you may be sabotaging your efforts. Luckily, this can be easily corrected using Thought Field Therapy techniques, and once mastered, these techniques take just seconds.

Out of all the exercises in this book, this following exercise is the most important one. No matter how effective any of the techniques are, they will only work if you actually do them! If you are Psychologically Reversed, you may talk yourself out of trying the exercises and thus sabotage your own efforts. By completing this exercise, you will ensure that you stay focused and positive.

I guarantee that if you complete the exercises relevant to you throughout this book, you will see a big difference; you may even get to like the new, more confident, you. I feel confident that you will feel much happier in yourself, and certainly tackle learning to drive with greater enthusiasm.

Are you Psychologically Reversed?

Although this exercise looks quite complicated when you first read it, don't be tempted to skip it, as it is imperative that you do it. Once you have mastered it, it only takes a few seconds, and is very effective. In addition to being used for increasing your confidence levels regarding learning to drive, you may also use it to increase your confidence levels generally, and address many other issues that you may experience.

You may have heard of two types of energy in nature: positive and negative (such as with electrical currents) and your body also has both positive and negative energy. If you are in negative polarity, you may unintentionally sabotage your attempts to increase your confidence, and this test will show if you are in negative or positive polarity. If the result comes out as negative, the technique will show you how to change to positive.

Testing yourself for Psychological Reversal

1. For this first part of the test, you need to find a willing partner. This first part asks you to calibrate your own strength with your partner. Stand upright and place one arm out directly to the side. Have your partner press firmly down on your outstretched arm just above the wrist; you need to resist this and hold your arm still. Notice how strong you feel, and the effort it takes you to resist. You need to assess just how much pressure you both need to exert for your arm to stay in the same position. If your partner is much stronger than you do not allow them to press so hard that you arm collapses. It is important your partner exerts a constant pressure, for about 3-4 seconds, without bouncing. They press, you resist.

2. Now place your other hand over the top of your head (but not touching) with the palm facing downwards. Ask your partner to apply the same pressure on the outstretched arm as before and see if your arm still stays in the same place or if it's weaker and your partner can push it down easily.

3. Next turn your hand over so the back of your hand is facing your head and the palm is facing up. Have your partner exert the same amount of pressure as before on your outstretched arm and resist.

You will probably notice a drastic difference between the two, in that with your palm facing your head your outstretched arm is strong, as this has 'positive polarity', and when you flip over so the back of your hand is facing your head your outstretched arm is weak, as this has 'negative polarity'. If this is the case then you are in 'positive polarity and are not Psychologically Reversed.

continued...

However, if both are the same strength, or it is the wrong way round, i.e. palm down is weak and palm up strong, it indicates a Psychological Reversal, and you are in 'negative polarity.'

In order to change to 'positive polarity', tap the side of your hand (where you would do a 'karate chop') 15-20 times and repeat the exercise; you should now find that you are in 'positive polarity'; that is your outstretched hand is strong when your other palm is facing your head, and weak when the back of your other hand is facing your head. This technique is reliable for almost everyone. Very occasionally, a person finds that they cannot feel a difference, and should this be the case, continue with the exercise as it may still be beneficial to you, but you may benefit from contacting a qualified Thought Field Therapist who can assist you further. (Contact details are at the back of the book).

Once you have identified a clear difference so that palm down is strong and palm up is weak, you can use this 'muscle testing' exercise to ask your body and your 'unconscious' mind questions. Now you have tested as above for Psychological Reversal, you need only to use the one outstretched arm for the following exercise, and need not place your other hand over the top of your head.

Place your arm out to the side, have your partner apply the same pressure for 3-4 seconds and say 'My name is ...' and give your correct name. While doing this you should resist and make a mental note of how strong your arm is. Rest for a few seconds then repeat, but this time say 'My name is daffy duck' and with your partner exerting the same pressure notice how weak your arm becomes in comparison to when you are telling the truth. This is a basic way of using Applied Kinesiology to see if you believe what you say. Once you are confident with the process, use it to test the statements in the following exercise.

Statement	Strong arm	Weak arm
I want to learn to drive with confidence	You genuinely want to learn to drive with confidence and are likely to be successful	On a deeper level, you do not want to learn how to drive with confidence and will sabotage your own attempts to learn to drive with confidence. Use the corrective treatment shown below and repeat until you can say the statement with a strong arm
I want to keep this lack of confidence whilst learning to drive	On a deeper level, you do not want to learn to drive and will sabotage your own attempts to learn to drive with confidence. Use the corrective treatment shown below and repeat until you can say the statement with a strong arm	You genuinely want to learn to drive with confidence and are likely to be successful

If the chart shows that you may sabotage your attempts to learn to drive with confidence, then use the following Corrective Treatment:

1. With your left hand, tap the side of your right hand (where you would do a karate chop) 15-20 times.

2. Tap the spot under your nose (just above your upper lip) 15-20 times.

3. With your right hand, tap the side of your left hand (where you would do a karate chop) 15-20 times.

Repeat the muscle test as shown in the chart. You should now get a strong arm response when you say 'I want to learn to drive with confidence', and a weak arm response when you say 'I want to keep this lack of confidence whilst learning to drive.'

If you still get a weak arm when you say 'I want to learn to drive with confidence', carry out the following exercise.

Staying out of Specific Psychological Reversal

With your left hand, tap the side of your right hand and repeat the following affirmations whilst focusing on wanting to learn to drive with confidence:

I want to be over the cause of this problem
I want to be completely over the cause of this problem
I will be over the cause of this problem
I will be completely over the cause of this problem
I want to be even better

Tap under your nose and repeat the above affirmations. With your right hand, tap the side of your left hand repeating the affirmations.

Repeat the muscle test with the statement 'I want to learn to drive with confidence'. You should now find that your arm is strong when you say this. This now means that you are not Psychologically Reversed to this concept, and this will make the rest of the exercises in the book much more effective. You will notice a huge difference in your performance and ability when your 'unconscious' mind is working with you, rather than against you.

Important daily exercise

In order to stay focused and positive, each morning, with your left hand, tap the side of your right hand and repeat the following affirmations (or whatever affirmations you feel most comfortable with, making sure they are very positive), whilst thinking about learning to drive with confidence.

**I want to learn to drive with confidence
I want to learn to drive with complete confidence
I will learn to drive with confidence
I will learn to drive with complete confidence
I want to be even better**

Tap under your nose and repeat the above affirmations. Then, with your right hand, tap the side of your left hand repeating the affirmations.

The great thing about Thought Field Therapy (TFT) is that it is very effective and has no side effects. This means if you are already positive and you use TFT, it does nothing, but if you have slipped into negative PR (as we all do at times) then it corrects it. This takes about a minute and can be done anywhere, anytime. Even without the affirmations, tapping the side of your hand regularly throughout the day whilst thinking about your confidence will help keep you positive and on track and help control any negative feelings of lack of confidence.

This exercise is effective for increasing your confidence levels whilst learning to drive and should you be experiencing difficulties and 'mental blocks' in specific areas, such as manoeuvres, hill starts, roundabouts, dual carriageways etc., you can use the above exercise for these as well. Just change your statement to something like: 'I want to be over the cause of this problem with roundabouts' (should get a strong arm response), and 'I want to keep this problem with roundabouts' (should get a weak arm response). Any other response is Psychological Reversal and you should perform the corrections as shown above.

As you discovered in Chapter Three, 'What makes a good driver?', it's important to have equal amounts of competence and confidence. You should now know if your levels are equal or not. If one is lacking, then you now have the tools at your disposal to correct the balance. Your next step is to read the chapters most relevant to you and to work through the exercises. This book contains all you need to help you pass your test stress-free and in fewer lessons, but it will only work if you are prepared to put some effort in yourself. This extra effort will take just five-ten minutes a day. However, the benefits you will gain will far outweigh the amount of effort required. Ask yourself now, are you ready for a completely new approach to passing your driving test? If so, then please read on.

Chapter Six

The basics

When you watch an experienced driver, much of what they do can be considered force of habit, in other words, using their unconscious mind. After a pattern repeats itself several times, we start to remember it; the more we do it, the stronger the association is, and therefore a new habit is formed. This is very useful when learning to drive.

The more that you do something the easier it gets. This may sound obvious, but it is something that you as a learner driver will often forget when you can't master a new skill straight away; you need to give yourself time to learn. The more that you repeat the new skill the more you will remember. If you want to learn quickly, you don't have to have a driving lesson everyday, but you do need to think about your driving every day. Throughout this chapter, you will find exercises designed to increase your learning capacity, without the need to take additional lessons, therefore giving you the opportunity to pass your driving test in fewer lessons.

Now for the science bit! When your brain experiences something new, such as learning to drive, it releases the chemical responsible for motivation called dopamine. Afterwards, the brain rewards you by releasing its 'happy' chemical, serotonin. Because this makes you feel happy, you are more motivated to try it again. Now, wouldn't it be wonderful if you could achieve this feeling between your driving lessons? The good news is that you can, and you will achieve this by following some very simple exercises.

It's just routine

If you have already taken a few lessons, you may be familiar with the MSPSL routine: Mirror, Signal, Position, Speed, Look. If you are very new to driving, your instructor will be explaining this to you on your first few lessons.

This routine forms the backbone of everything you do whilst driving, including dealing with junctions, dual carriageways, and hazards, etc.

The most effective way that we can learn a new habit is to practice it as often as possible. However, if you only spend one hour a week learning to drive, then you won't have the opportunity to encourage this habit to form quickly. You can liken learning to drive to learning the words to a song. If you listen to a song on the radio just once every week, it will take you a very long time to learn the words. However, if you hear the song repeatedly, you will be able to remember the words after just a short time. Unless of course you have your own vehicle, or are taking an intensive driving course, you cannot physically drive for hours every day until the skill is imbedded in your subconscious. This is where your imagination can help immensely, and enable you to speed up the learning process.

When you first start learning to drive, your focus is understandably very much on what's happening in the car, such as where your feet go, how to steer, where the gearlever is etc. It's hard to remember, especially when you first start your lessons and if you are only driving for one hour per week, to do things in the correct order. Even when getting close to test standard, many pupils still do things in the wrong order. Instructors find that they still have to remind even experienced pupils to check their mirrors before slowing down, signalling or changing direction. Later in this chapter, you will find techniques that will help you to easily recall the information that you have learnt during your lesson. This in turn will have two beneficial effects. Firstly, your instructor won't have to keep repeating the same instructions, and secondly, as a result, you will progress much more quickly than you thought possible.

MSPSL

The mirror, signal, position, speed, look routine will eventually become second nature to you when you have been driving for a while, however this is of little help to you when you first start to learn, and it feels like you are having to remember everything all at once. As I have stated previously, this book is not intended as a driving manual; that is what your driving instructor is for, however, at this point, I think that it's helpful to recap why the MSPSL routine is so important. As with many things in life, if you understand the reasoning behind something, then you are more likely to remember the importance of it.

It's as easy as riding a bike!

Before we look at this routine in more detail, it may be helpful if we relate it to something that you may already be familiar with, such as riding a bicycle. So, let's look at turning right from the main road onto a side road. You look over your right shoulder to check that it is clear to move to the centre of the road; you would then put your right arm out to inform traffic that you are about to change your direction, after which you cycle to the centre of the road in order to make your turn. You then slow your speed down, perhaps change the gear on your bike, check that it is clear to go, then cycle across the road.

Now, let's try it in the car!

In those terms it sounds very easy. Making the turn in the car is exactly the same. Firstly, you would check your appropriate **mirrors**, and then you apply your right **signal**. After that, if it is clear to go, you **position** your vehicle to just left of the centre line, slow your **speed** down, and change gear if necessary, and finally **look** where you are going. This describes the **mirror, signal, position, speed, look** routine. When put like this, ask yourself does it now seems that bit easier to understand, and therefore to remember?

Importance of correct order

Often a pupil will remember what to do, but not in the correct order. This is often the case with learners who are dyslexic as they may experience issues with short-term memory and sequencing. If you are dyslexic, you will find some wonderful advice in Chapter Nine, 'Dyslexic and dyspraxic dilemma'. Unfortunately, forgetting the correct sequence can be just as dangerous as forgetting part of the routine. It's critically important that the routine is followed in the correct order. If you have already had some lessons, ask yourself how often you have found yourself braking before remembering to check your mirrors and put your signal on?

Now we are going to look at the MSPSL routine in more detail, and discuss why it's so important to remember it in the correct order. However, it's no use to you to know it if you can't remember it, so after that I will help you to learn how to remember the correct order easily every lesson, and hopefully this will enable you to learn to drive in fewer repetitive lessons.

This may appear very mundane to you, and you will probably be tempted to skip this section, but I urge you to read it, even if you are an experienced learner. I make no apologies for spending time on this routine. As any driving instructor will tell you, countless numbers of people fail their driving tests as a result of forgetting the MSPSL routine on their driving test.

Mirror check

Your instructor will instil in you the importance of mirror checks before changing your speed, signalling or changing direction. This is because you need to have an awareness of what's happening around you before you change your direction or speed. For example, when intending to make a right turn, if you move your car across the road to make the turn before checking your mirrors, then you could potentially cause an accident with perhaps a motorcyclist who is overtaking you. Therefore, your instructor will advise you always to check your interior mirror before you make a move followed by the exterior mirror of the direction that you are intending to go.

Another example of appropriate mirror checks is when you are approaching traffic lights. If you are checking your mirrors regularly, you will see how close the vehicle following you is. If the traffic light has been on green for a while, you know that it may turn red just as you get there. However, if the vehicle behind is quite close to you (tailgating), then it is advisable to ease off the accelerator so if you did have to brake, then you could do so in a more gradual manner, thus giving the driver behind more time to react. I have had pupils comment to me that 'it's his own fault if he runs into the back of me', but that's no consolation if you or your passengers are injured, or the driver who causes the accident is uninsured and your vehicle is damaged, with no one to pay for it.

Perhaps you will now see the relevance of checking your mirrors before slowing down, but often it's more difficult to understand why the need to check the mirrors before speeding up. Consider leaving a 30 mph limit and entering a 60 mph limit.

Try to imagine the consequences if a car following you decided to overtake you whilst you were speeding up, and there was a vehicle approaching from the opposite direction. If you hadn't noticed that he was overtaking you, you would have a very dangerous situation.

Finally, we will look at mirror checks when leaving a roundabout. When you are on the roundabout, you have priority over traffic emerging from the left, however, if you don't check your mirrors and to the left when leaving a roundabout, if a car emerging hasn't seen you, or perhaps an emergency services vehicle may need access to the roundabout quickly there could be a collision. If you don't check, you won't be able to anticipate this will you?

How can mirror checks show your instructor or examiner how good your planning and awareness is?

Mirror checks play another important part in learning to drive and the driving test. Because a mirror check should be the **very first** thing that you do prior to signalling, changing speed and/or direction, for example negotiating a junction or hazard, your driving instructor or examiner will watch you to check that you are using the mirrors at the appropriate times.

If I see a parked car up ahead, and I don't see my pupil checking their mirrors to see if it is safe to go past, then I don't know if they have spotted the hazard or not. Therefore, I am on my guard as I am anticipating that they have not spotted the hazard. However, if the pupil checks the mirrors in plenty of time, I know that they are aware of the situation and planning to deal with it safely. When you check your mirrors this is your fist 'signal' to the instructor or examiner that you are aware of what's happening around you, and that you are planning appropriate action.

Although your instructor may know that you are a good driver, the first time that the examiner will see you drive is on your driving test. If you are not checking your mirrors and therefore not aware of what's happening around you, then you are not creating a very good impression of a safe, competent, confident, considerate driver and you will not pass your test. Whereas if you check your mirrors in plenty of time, and act on what you see, then you are creating a good impression, and the examiner will feel more relaxed, as you are showing him or her that you are in control.

There is more about use of mirrors and planning and awareness in Chapter Fourteen, 'The top ten reasons for failure and how to avoid them', so I suggest you to read this as you progress through your lessons. I hope that you will now see the relevance of appropriate mirror checks, and make sure that you always make full use of them when driving to protect yourself and others from harm.

Signal

As other motorists won't see you check your mirrors, your signal should be the first indication to them that you intend to do something, such as make a turn, leave a roundabout, or pull up at the side of the road. However, if you get the order wrong and brake before signalling, this will give the incorrect message to the traffic around you. How often have you been in a car and the vehicle in front has braked and you've wondered what the driver's up to? Then, at the last moment, you see his indicator. If the following driver sees your indicator, this should mean that he backs off because he's then expecting to see your brake lights. This is therefore why it's imperative to make sure that you check your mirrors and then signal **before** braking or changing direction.

Position

Once you have checked that it's safe to make the turn etc., and you've informed other motorists that you are about to make a turn by your signal, then it's time to take up the correct road position. You need to make sure that you follow the correct order, rather than just taking up a new road position without checking your mirrors or signalling your intention to other motorists.

Speed

When faced with having to make a turn, negotiate a roundabout, or deal with a hazard, because a pupil is often nervous about getting the correct speed and gear, they will tend to brake and perhaps change gear before thinking of anything else. So often, as soon as a pupil is given an instruction such as: 'take the next turn on the left', their foot will go to the brake and their hand will go to the gearlever, prior to checking their mirrors and signalling. Therefore, it's imperative that before braking (unless in an emergency of course, but your instructor will discuss this with you), you must check your mirrors and signal if necessary. You are then giving following traffic plenty of time to react.

When you are first learning to drive, your instructor will give you directions earlier than they would with a more experienced pupil, to give you time to assimilate the information, and to carry out the correct procedure. If your instructor does give you late directions, and you panic as a result, ask them to give the directions earlier, to give you more time to react to their request, and carry out the sequence in the correct order.

Look

This may seem obvious, but it is very common for learners to try to make a turn or emerge at a roundabout resulting in the instructor having to stop them because it is not safe to go. You need always to make sure that it is safe to go before committing yourself to action. (There is more information on judging when to go in Chapter Fourteen, 'The top ten reasons for failure and how to avoid them'.)

Now you understand the principle, how can you remember it all, and in the correct order?

Now that you know the reasons behind the MSPSL routine, you can understand the importance and relevance of getting the correct order. So now we will look at how you can do this. As I mentioned earlier, the imagination is a powerful tool and can help you immensely. If you just have one driving lesson per week, without using the power of your imagination you are more than likely to forget much of what you have been taught by the next lesson. The following exercises will help you to remember, and to make the learning process more fun and enjoyable. If you are dyslexic, I know that you may have a problem with short-term memory, and sequencing, so learning this routine may prove quite a challenge for you. The exercises below are helpful, but you will benefit from reading Chapter Nine, 'Dyslexic and dyspraxic dilemma' where you will find 'multi-sensory learning techniques' which will make the learning process even easier, and believe me, much more enjoyable. Try the following exercises.

Repeat your driving lesson time after time...

After your driving lesson, you don't want to just forget about what you have learnt in that lesson until the next one! As soon as you have opportunity after your lesson, go through everything that you can remember in your head and try to recall as much of what your instructor told you as possible. Re run the image of the things that you did, and if you made mistakes on the lesson, think to yourself: 'If I could go back and do it again, how would I do it differently'. Everyone has thought at one time or another; 'If only I could go back and change...' By going through this simple exercise, you are encouraging your mind to recall the data.

For instance, if you have carried out the MSPSL routine twenty times in your lesson, by frequently recalling the lesson, your brain will believe that you have done it many more times. This has two beneficial effects. Firstly, you are helping to create more associations in your mind, and therefore, it will recall the data much more effectively. Secondly, you are thinking of what you would have done differently, and therefore programming your mind to do it the correct way on future lessons.

'Modelling' your behaviour...

There is a variation of this exercise in Chapter Twelve, 'Are you talking yourself into failure?', which you will find useful as you progress in your lessons, especially if you are experiencing difficulty in any particular area. Here, we are using it to help you learn the basics.

If you watch a task being performed correctly, it is much easier to learn to do it yourself. This exercise is designed to enable you to visualise yourself driving as well as an experienced driver. You need to pick as your role model someone whom you not only admire but someone who is a competent driver. You may wish to watch your parents, partner or friend, or better still, ask your driving instructor for a demonstration. Your driving instructor is the best person to model yourself on for correct technique.

For this exercise to be most effective, you not only need to copy the physical actions, but also to think how your role model would think. For example, if you are watching your instructor performing a left turn, the physical aspects that you will notice is that they check their appropriate mirrors, signal, position the car to the left, choose the appropriate gear, and make the turn. In addition, you need to be aware of your instructor's thought processes involved in making the turn. The more realistic you make the visualisation, the more effective and beneficial the exercise.

1. Imagine your chosen role model performing the action that you want to perfect. Make sure that you remember in detail everything that they do. Run through the memory several times until you can remember it perfectly.

continued...

2. Imagine yourself as your role model; imagine sitting in the driving seat in the same relaxed posture that they have. See what they would see, and feel the same sense of confidence that they would have.

3. Repeatedly run through this memory in your mind, imagining yourself performing the action in exactly the same way as your role model. Keep visualising until you can picture yourself performing the action with the same confidence and ability as your role model.

4. Repeat this exercise as many times as you want, and for as many scenarios as you want, until you can picture yourself performing with as much confidence and competence as your instructor, or chosen role model.

If you have difficulty visualising, try the technique in Chapter Seven, 'Mastering the manoeuvres' as this will reinforce your ability to visualise you performing at your peak.

Force of habit!

Habits are hard to break, whether they are good or bad. How often have you heard an experienced driver say: 'I'm glad that I've not got to take my test again. I'd never pass; I have too many bad habits'? I had been driving for many years before I trained to be a driving instructor, and I also had lots of habits that I found difficult to change as they were so deeply entrenched after so many years. However, habits aren't necessarily a bad thing, but whether they are good or bad, they are very hard to break. That's why it's important when learning to drive to instill good habits early on, such as checking the mirrors, but put a stop to bad habits, such as looking at the gearlever, before they become so firmly entrenched that it becomes very difficult to break them.

If you do have bad habits, however, all is not lost. If I can become a qualified driving instructor after so many years of bad habits, then I'm sure that any habits that that you may have fallen into can be easily rectified. We will consider two habits, one good one bad, and the positive or negative consequences of having these habits.

Someone's moved the gearlever! A habit to break

When you first learn to drive, you may feel that you have to look where the gears are, but after a few lessons there should be no need for this. Having said that, I have taught many pupils who came to me supposedly at 'test standard', who still looked down at the gearlever when changing gear, and especially when they stopped and selected first gear. During the course of their lessons, they would have selected first gear countless times, so they shouldn't need to check where the gearlever is because it's still in the same place as the last time that they looked at it; it hasn't miraculously moved since the last gear change!

However, this is the problem with a bad habit; the pupil doesn't actually need to look at the gearlever, as they know where it is, but it's still habit from when they first started learning to drive. If you do know where the gearlever is, but have the habit of checking just to make sure that it's still there, try the next exercise now, and the exercises 'Replacement activity' and 'Linking actions' on your next and subsequent lessons.

Picturing the gearlever
Do this exercise now

As you learned from the two previous exercises, visualisation is a very powerful tool, and particularly so for learning the position of the gears. For this exercise you need to try shutting your eyes and picturing the gearlever in the car that you drive.

Picture where the first, second, third, fourth and maybe fifth gears are. Picture also reverse gear.

Once you can picture these clearly, imagine yourself changing gear easily whilst looking in your mirror.
Play around in your imagination going back and forth between all the gears so you can do it easily and without much thought.

If you do this several times before your next lesson, you should find that you are able to change gear easily whilst being aware of what's happening around you, rather than concentrating on the gear change itself. Remember, if you pictured 100 gear changes, your subconscious mind thinks that you actually did those gear changes.

Replacement activity
Do this exercise on your next
and subsequent lessons

During your driving lesson, whenever you have to negotiate a junction, roundabout etc., scan the road on approach to see if it's safe to go, whilst at the same time selecting the correct gear. This is a replacement activity; whilst you are doing something else, you aren't thinking of looking at the gearlever. Also, this makes your drive flow more because if you are scanning the junction on approach, you are not stopping unnecessarily. (If you are still quite new to driving and your instructor is advising you of the appropriate gear, I recommend that you still carry out this exercise, as you should have learnt on your early lessons where each gear is and should be able to change gear without looking.)

'Linking' actions
Do this exercise on your next
and subsequent lessons

Whenever you need to change gear during your driving lesson, make the effort to link the gear change to a mirror check.

These last two exercises benefit you in two ways; firstly, they will help you to break a bad habit by giving you a replacement activity, and secondly, the replacement activity will actually improve your driving by increasing your awareness, and improving the efficiency with which you deal with junctions, as well as giving you increased awareness of what's happening around you because you are checking your mirrors more frequently.

The unconscious mind remembers two or more things that we do close together. When a pattern has been repeated several times, the actions are linked. Therefore, it won't take long for your unconscious mind to link a gear change to a mirror check, or scanning the junction on approach.

Positive versus negative instruction

You may have noticed that in the above exercises I've not suggested that you think to yourself: **'I must not look at my gears'**; instead, I've given you something else to do at the same time. This is because your mind does not work in negatives. In order to think about not looking at your gears, you have to think about looking at them; in a similar way this is like a parent saying to a small child, 'don't knock your drink off the table', and the child will first think of knocking it off the table before they try to think of not knocking it off the table.

Therefore, it's important when carrying out any visualisation exercises that you think in 'positives' and not 'negatives'. It's easy as an instructor to fall into the trap of telling pupils what **not** to do, but it's much more constructive to give instruction in a positive manner. Take note of how your instructor teaches you; a good instructor will be very positive. Look at the following examples of different methods of instruction:

- 'Don't look at the gearlever', compared with, 'Check your mirror when changing gear'.

- 'Don't take your foot off the clutch so quickly', compared with, 'Ease your foot slowly off the clutch'.

- 'Don't do the manoeuvre so quickly', compared with, 'When performing a manoeuvre, do it slowly as this will give you greater control'.

- 'Don't brake so harshly', compared with, 'Brake gently and progressively'.

With each of the former 'negative' instructions, your brain remembers what **not** to do, therefore making it much harder for you to remember what you should be doing. With each of the latter 'positive' instructions, your brain is 're-wiring' itself to remember the positive instructions permanently.

I want to offer a final caution against looking at your gearlever; during your driving test, the examiner will expect you to know where the gearlever is and what gear you are in, and will not consider that you are a 'test standard' candidate if you need to look at the gears.

The best habit ever
A habit to keep

Appropriate mirror checks are one of the best habits to form early on in your lessons. If you get into the habit of checking your mirrors from the beginning, this good habit will stay with you, and as with looking at the gearlever, will be a hard habit to break, which in this case is good.

If you are just starting to learn to drive, listen to what your instructor says and try to develop good habits from the start. If you have been driving for a while and have started to develop bad habits, as you now know, this is counter productive, not only to passing your driving test in fewer lessons, but also for safe driving for life. Therefore, I suggest you use the exercises throughout this chapter to ensure that you develop and retain good habits.

Remember that if you are trying to erase a bad habit, such as looking at the gearlever, taking your foot too quickly off the clutch and stalling, or letting the wheel slip through your hands, then instead of thinking about **not** having that behaviour that you want to eradicate, you need to turn it into a positive thought. Take for example letting the steering wheel slip through your hands.

Rather than thinking: 'I mustn't let the wheel slip through my hands', change your mental picture to one of visualising steering perfectly and feeding the wheel correctly through your hands. You are therefore reinforcing the positive image each and every time that you picture something the correct way, and reducing the negative effect of the bad habit.

If you are already an experienced learner, you will know the importance of appropriate mirror checks. If however, you are new to learning to drive, then hopefully this chapter will have given you an insight into the importance of the MSPSL routine and the necessity of carrying it out in the correct order. Missed mirror checks, not acting on the information or lack of observation accounts for six out of ten test failures. Therefore, I suggest that you take time to read Chapter Fourteen, 'The top ten reasons for failure and how to avoid them'.

There are now a few blank pages for you and/or your instructor to write or draw (whichever you find the easiest method of remembering) the mirror, signal, position, speed, look routine. You will find the multi-sensory learning techniques in Chapter Nine, 'Dyslexic and dyspraxic dilemma' helpful for this exercise.

A note of caution: if you complete this exercise then don't intend to look at it until your next lesson, then there was not much point in buying the book! Promise yourself that you will look at it every day. You don't have to spend ages, just a minute or so, so it becomes etched

into your subconscious. You will find that after just a little while 'The basics' become second nature, and you can perform them as naturally as you would make a cup of tea, leaving your conscious mind free to perform all the other necessities whilst driving.

The good news is that you can use the above exercises for whatever you are working on with your instructor to learn stress free, more quickly and easily, therefore saving you money on repetitive lessons.

Pupil/Instructor notes

Pupil/Instructor notes

Pupil/Instructor notes

Chapter Seven

Mastering the manoeuvres

Nine out of ten manoeuvres performed correctly is good, but not good enough if the one that you get wrong is the one you perform on your test!

After you have started to get to grips with driving forward, your instructor will throw a spanner in the works; he will suddenly expect you to go backwards as well. Every single manoeuvre features in the top ten reasons for failure published by Driving Standards Agency, and getting it right nine times out of ten is no good if the one time you get it wrong is on your test. It may seem unfair as that's the equivalent of asking a tennis player to hit an ace every time, a snooker player to pot every ball, or a darts player to consistently hit double top, but remember:

there are no second chances when it comes to your driving test

It is important therefore that you are capable of performing every manoeuvre correctly. You are allowed one forward 'shunt' on each manoeuvre which should hopefully be enough allow you to correct yourself, but if not, then you can say goodbye to your test pass, even if you haven't done anything else wrong on your test. When you read Chapter Fourteen, 'The top ten reasons for failure and how to avoid them', you will find that every manoeuvre features on this list. The exercises in this chapter will improve your ability to get every manoeuvre right every time.

Why do I have to do them anyway?

At the time of writing, Driving Standards Agency are evaluating the current driving test, and the manoeuvres will be one of the things under discussion. Pupils often question the necessity of manoeuvres and say 'I'll never do that once I've passed my test'. If you think this way, ask yourself, what happens when you want to park at the supermarket or outside your house on the road? If your friend lives in a cul-de-sac are you going to abandon your vehicle because you can't perform a turn in the road? Of course not, so it's essential that you learn to do the manoeuvres regardless of whether you are going to be tested on them or not.

However, if you find them difficult, you are not alone; just go to your local supermarket on a Saturday afternoon and watch people try to park in the marked bays. You will see people driving around the car park looking for a space that they can drive forward into because they can't reverse into a bay. You may find it very interesting, and I would suggest that you take sandwiches and a flask of coffee, as it's a lot more entertaining than watching the television!

Many drivers have difficulty with the parallel park. You have probably seen countless drivers try to get into a space, only to shunt forward and backwards many times, often running up and down the kerb, frequently abandoning parking their car at all and driving on to find a larger space. Do you want to end up like these drivers, or do you want to Master those Manoeuvres and perform them with accuracy and confidence?

'So, which way do I turn the wheel again?'

It's amazing how many people who are competent going forwards appear to lose all driving ability when reversing. It's not surprising because we probably spend about ninety-nine percent of our time going forwards, and one percent reversing. On countless occasions I've had to remind a pupil which way to turn the wheel when reversing. Instructors have a variety of methods to help you remember; I always find it useful to explain, and then show my pupils to steer the same way in reverse as when going forwards, i.e., when you want to go left towards the kerb going forwards, do the same whilst reversing. It may sound silly, but try sitting on a bike, turn the handle bars left and walk it forwards, then walk the bike backwards and see which way it goes. The exercises below will help you to remember this.

The manoeuvres are a necessity, and if you are lucky, you may find that you take to them very quickly. It's more likely though that you will find some of them quite difficult to begin with, and it can be very frustrating trying to get them right. What pupils tend to find most demoralising about manoeuvres is the lack of consistency, they find they are able to do one perfectly, whilst the next one is nowhere near as good. As you read at the beginning of this chapter, getting the manoeuvre right nine times out of ten is no good if the one you get wrong is the one that you do on your driving test.

In order for you to gain the most benefit from this section, you may want to ask your instructor for their help. You will find that your instructor has their own method of teaching each of the manoeuvres, and they may well give you advice on 'turning points' etc. which can be specific to the vehicle that you are learning in. Therefore, I have not given any detailed instructions as it's best that you stick to the method you are familiar with, thus maintaining consistency. My aim in this chapter is to give you exercises that you can use between lessons to improve your memory of how to perform the manoeuvre and therefore improve the probability of getting it right on your next lesson, thus saving you both time and money, and making your instructor's life a lot easier.

Testing yourself for 'Specific Reversal' to learning the manoeuvres

As you discovered in Chapter Five, 'Your baseline confidence level', it may be that you are 'Specifically Reversed' to mastering the manoeuvres. You can test yourself for this by following the 'Specific Reversal' exercise that you did in Chapter Five, but replacing the statement 'I want to learn to drive with confidence' with 'I want to perform the manoeuvres accurately and with confidence', then complete the rest of the exercise to ensure that you are not specifically reversed. You will find that you feel much more positive about learning the manoeuvres after this exercise.

'Model' yourself on the expert - Your instructor!

I discussed in Chapter Six, 'The basics', the benefits of 'modelling' your actions on those of a role-model, and this is a particularly useful exercise for mastering the manoeuvres. Some instructors take the view that the best form of teaching is explanation, and that demonstration is only to be used when absolutely necessary or when nothing else has worked. I take the opposite view, and frequently demonstrate manoeuvres etc. to my pupils. My belief is that if you watch something being performed correctly, it is much easier to learn to do it yourself. This exercise is designed to enable you to visualise yourself performing the manoeuvre as well as your instructor.

For this exercise to be most effective, you not only need to copy the physical actions, but also to think how your role model would think. For example, if you are watching your instructor performing a turn in the road, note how they physically perform the manoeuvre, but also be aware of your instructor's thought processes involved in performing the manoeuvre. The more realistic you make the visualisation, the more effective and beneficial the exercise.

When your instructor is introducing you to a new manoeuvre, I suggest that you ask your instructor to perform the manoeuvre a couple of times so that you have a clear picture of how it is done. Then ask your instructor if you can do the exercise that follows. It only takes a couple of minutes but the time it saves in the long run makes it well worth while. If your instructor thinks that this is a bit odd, ask them to read this exercise so they understand the reason for you wanting to do the exercise on your lesson. If you find that your instructor isn't happy about using your lesson time doing 'silly, pointless' exercises, I suggest that you ask your instructor to read 'Note for ADIs' at the beginning of the book. He or she may then be more amenable to your trying the exercises.

'Model' Manoeuvres

1. Imagine your chosen role model performing the manoeuvre that you require help with. Make sure that you remember in detail everything that they do. Run through the memory several times until you can remember it perfectly.

2. Imagine yourself as your role model; sit in the driving seat in the same relaxed posture that your instructor has. See what they would see, and feel the same sense of confidence that they would have.

3. Repeatedly run through this memory in your mind, imagining yourself performing the manoeuvre in exactly the same way as your instructor. Keep visualising until you can picture yourself performing the manoeuvre with the same confidence and ability as your instructor.

4. If you repeat this exercise a couple of times directly after your instructor has given you a demonstration, you will find it much easier to perform the manoeuvre when you come to try it.

5. To reinforce the memory, make sure that you run through this visualisation exercise a few times as soon after your lesson as you are able. Use this exercise for as many manoeuvres as you want, until you can picture yourself performing with as much confidence and competence as your instructor, or chosen role model.

Many people find the above exercise very beneficial and can easily 'picture' themselves in the same confident manner as their instructor, and as a result of this, improve their manoeuvres immensely. However, not all people find visualising easy. This next exercise is designed to help you visualise performing at your peak. I have put this exercise in this chapter, as I have found that the manoeuvres tend to be the hardest thing that learners have to do. However, you can use it for anything; just substitute trying to visualise the manoeuvre with whatever you require help with. The first part of the exercise seems a little silly, but it's important to discover how well you are able to visualise something, as after you have completed the exercise you will be able to ascertain how effective it was.

Visualisation for 'Peak Performance'

1. Shut your eyes, and picture in your 'mind's eye' an apple. On a scale of 1-10, how easy is it to visualise where 1 is easy and 10 difficult?

2. Imagine the apple doing something strange, like floating through the air. Now, hold onto the apple and picture yourself floating a little way above the ground whilst holding the apple. On a scale of 1-10, how easy is this to visualise?

3. If you managed to picture that quite easily, you have proved that you are capable of visualisation. Next I want you to visualise how you would normally carry out a manoeuvre that you find difficult. Try to feel the same tension and anxiety that you would normally feel, and where you normally go wrong, and perhaps the feeling of inadequacy that you cannot perform the manoeuvre correctly. Rate this again on a scale of 1 to 10, where 1 is easy to picture it going wrong and 10 is hard to picture it going wrong. Don't worry if you found this quite easy to picture as this is the case for most people as every time that you have had difficulty performing a manoeuvre, your brain stores it, rather like a computer.

---

continued...

4. Next imagine yourself performing the manoeuvre with as much ease, accuracy and ability as your driving instructor. Try to feel the same sense of confidence that your instructor would feel. Rate this on a scale of 1-10 where 1 is easy to visualise and 10 is hard to visualise. It's likely that you will find it harder to visualise doing it well rather than badly. The next actions are going to help you to visualise yourself performing the manoeuvre easily and accurately.

5. Use the Basic Tapping Sequence for 'visualisation for peak performance', in Chapter One, 'How to use this book' and follow the procedure described. You may find that you are able to 'picture' yourself performing the manoeuvre to the required standard after just carrying out this exercise once. However, if you don't feel totally confident, repeat the exercise in full a few more times until you do feel utterly confident. You can then keep going through this exercise with each manoeuvre that you want to improve.

Approach each manoeuvre with 'a clean slate'

You may find that you carry the emotional 'baggage' of previous manoeuvres going wrong, especially if you have failed a test as a result of not getting a manoeuvre correct. It's disheartening to keep thinking, 'If only....' because then every time that you try the manoeuvre in the future, you will think of the previous failed attempts at getting it correct.

I would suggest that if every time your instructor asks you to perform a manoeuvre, you think this way, using the **Basic Tapping Sequence** for 'eliminating past traumas and upset' in Chapter One, 'How to use this book', will benefit you immensely. You may also find the **Basic Tapping Sequence**s for 'anxiety and stress', and 'frustration and impatience' useful. Try the different sequences and find which one is most effective for you. This exercise will help you to rid the negative feelings that you have towards manoeuvres, allowing you to perform them with a clean slate, without the negative emotional attachment. You need to perform the exercise whilst focusing intently on all the negative feeling that you attach to the particular manoeuvre.

'I'm not frustrated....'

As I mentioned earlier, one of the most annoying aspects of the manoeuvres is the fact that you may get one correct, then mess up the next one. This usually leads to a great deal of frustration, which in turn leads to anger at yourself because of your lack of consistence; therefore you can again use the Basic Tapping Sequence for 'frustration and impatience'.

And finally....

The biggest problem that pupils face with manoeuvres is the necessity to perform them accurately and on demand such as on their driving test. The exercises in this chapter, if performed on a regular basis, will enable you to master the manoeuvres much more easily. The crucial point here is the necessity to perform the exercises regularly, and the visualisation exercise on a daily basis. As discussed previously, learning a new skill is much easier if done repeatedly; like learning the words to a song. However, spending perhaps just fifteen minutes a week on a manoeuvre is hardly conducive to mastering it easily. Therefore, I urge you to spend a few minutes each day performing the exercises which you find most beneficial.

Even if you are not dyslexic, it will be useful for you to read Chapter Nine ,'Dyslexic and dyspraxic dilemma', as it has lots of helpful hints and tips for you and your instructor to follow which will help you to perform the manoeuvres accurately. This chapter discusses 'multi-sensory learning', i.e. using more of your senses than you may normally use, to facilitate more effective and speedy learning. Ask your instructor to read this chapter with you, as you may find that some of the advice is helpful especially for learning the manoeuvres.

Below there are a few blank pages for you and your instructor to write or draw (whichever you find the easiest method of remembering) the manoeuvres that you need to learn. You will find the multi-sensory learning techniques in Chapter Nine, 'Dyslexic and dyspraxic dilemma' helpful for this exercise.

A note of caution: if you complete this exercise then don't attempt to look at it until your next lesson, there was not much point in buying the book! Promise yourself

that you will look at it every day. You don't have to
spend a great deal of time, just a minute or so, long
enough for it to become etched into your subconscious.
You will find that on your next lesson, you will be able to
perform them much more easily. Also, if your instructor
doesn't return to the same manoeuvre for a few lessons,
if you have been doing the exercises in this chapter,
then you will amaze them by still remembering how to
do them.

Pupil/Instructor notes

Pupil/Instructor notes

Pupil/Instructor notes

Chapter Eight

How much is your
personality costing you?

This may sound like an odd question, but as you are aware, we all have different personalities and our personalities can work to either help or hinder our progress when learning to drive. For example, ask yourself whether you are the type of person that doesn't like to give in and will try and try until you get something right, or do you get frustrated really easily if you don't get something right first time, or are you really laid back and don't care how slowly or quickly you pass your test?

Even though no personality is inherently good or bad, each personality does have good and bad attributes. Therefore, in your driving you need to use the good attributes of your personality to your advantage, and make sure that you work on your bad attributes to minimise their negative effect. For example, if you are a perfectionist, this is good because it means that you will work with dedication when learning to drive until you get it right, but the bad aspect is that you can get very bogged down in minute detail that may not be really relevant. On the other hand, if you are the sort of person who tends to fake it on the day, then the good aspect of your personality is that you won't be worked up or worried about your approaching test. However, you may not put your utmost effort into learning, because you believe that you can just fake it on the day.

Although each one of us may have a predominant characteristic, you are likely to find that you relate to more than one of the personalities listed below, and I would suggest that you take on board the suggestions relevant to you, as it may ultimately save you a lot of time and money.

The Perfectionist

It will depend on the nature of the challenge and your dedication to a task whether you tend to stick at it or quit it. If the task is important to you and you are dedicated, you may find that you become a *Perfectionist Sticker* and stubbornly refuse to move on until you master the task to perfection. If on the other hand you don't get it right first time, you may get very frustrated with yourself and become a *Perfectionist Quitter* and give up before you have given yourself chance to master the task. I know from personal experience that both of these characteristics can cause problems, and below you will find examples of this personality type, and how to use it to your best advantage.

The Perfectionist Quitter

A few years ago when I bought the Rally Challenge play station game, my partner Dave, who is also a driving instructor, was having great fun tearing around, not caring whether the car went off the track or not. If he did, he just got back on again and kept going even though bits were starting to fall off the car. He eventually got to the end of the race, with the slowest time and a car that looked like it had done the rounds at the dodgems, but he kept practicing until he eventually won.

However, this is not how my personality made me behave. As soon as something went wrong with the game, regardless of whether I was at the beginning or near the end of the race, I stopped that race and started at the beginning again. I couldn't see the point in continuing if I knew that I wasn't going to win. Therefore, I never did finish the race, because I was asking too much of myself too soon. As Dave was willing to persevere, even when he wasn't very good at it, he became really good at Rally Challenge. I, on the

other hand, just ended up with a broken console after I
threw it at the wall, as I was so angry that I couldn't get it
right first time! The consequence was that because I wasn't
perfect to start with, I didn't persevere, and I never did
learn to be any good at play station games.

**Do you throw your toys out of the pram when
you can't get something right first time?**

I learned to drive about twenty-five years ago, and I had
the same personality traits back then as I do today. I
had row after row with my Mum and Dad because at the
slightest error I would 'throw my toys out of the pram'. As
a result, they both refused to go out driving with me until I
had had some proper driving lessons.

You may have had a similar experience; if you get into
arguments with your parents or partner when they are
trying to teach you to drive, it's usually because you are
too close in your relationship, and are therefore used to
venting your frustration out on each other.

In contrast, your driving instructor is trained to be
professional in all circumstances, and although they should
be friendly and approachable, they will maintain a more
detached relationship from you than that which you have
with family or friends. Therefore, they should have a
calming influence on you. If they don't, and make you feel
just as worked up, or they get angry with you, then perhaps
you should consider changing your instructor.

The Perfectionist Sticker

If you fit into this personality, and the task is very
important to you, you will feel immense dedication and
commitment to it, and if you are a *Perfectionist Sticker,*

you will most likely take the challenge to the point of obsession and the exclusion of everything else.

It is very difficult to alter our own basic personalities, but it is good to be aware of what our characteristics are and rather than try to change them, try to work with them to our advantage. If you have a personality like mine, it's very hard not to get frustrated if you can't master a new skill straight away. I have always wanted to learn to speak French, and to this end, I obtained an eight-hour course in French on CD. As I was much more dedicated to learning to speak French than mastering the play station, I refused to go onto the next CD until I was totally fluent with the current one.

The outcome is that I now know my French course inside out, but it took me a whole year to work through eight CDs. That's over six weeks to work through a one hour CD! If you apply this way of thinking to learning to drive, it would cost thousands of pounds to get to the stage of being ready to take the test.

I teach many people who are like me; if they keep stalling, or cannot get the hang of reversing around a corner straight away, they get very frustrated with themselves. The outcome of this is usually one of two things; either they want to persist at the same thing until they get it right, becoming obsessive about it, or they just end up that worked up that they want to quit because they can't get it right straight away. Either response is not helpful when learning to drive.

How to work with this personality type to your advantage

So, what can you do if you fall into either of these Perfectionist categories? From my own experience, I've found that it is essential you set yourself **realistic goals.** You can apply this technique to anything, not just learning to drive. For example, on my day off, I may decide that I want to walk the dogs, get the washing done, clear the cars out, paint the sitting room etc., and then at the end of the day find that I'm angry and frustrated with myself because I haven't managed to get it all done. At the start of the day, I failed to set myself realistic goals.

There are many good books on the market about goal setting, but the principle is quite simple as far as learning to drive is concerned. Discuss with your instructor what you would both hope to achieve by the end of each lesson. Let's say for example that you are attempting to reverse round a corner for the first time; it's unrealistic to expect you to be able to perform the manoeuvre perfectly on your first attempt. A more realistic goal would perhaps be to be able to determine your turning point, keep slow control with your clutch, and have quite good observation, but to require assistance from your instructor with regards to improving your observation, and determining the amount of steering required, and when to straighten up. By setting yourself a goal that is more realistic, you can remind yourself that you don't have to be perfect straight away, and to be pleased at achieving the goal that you and your instructor have set.

Realistic goal setting is a helpful technique for the Perfectionist Quitter. If you fit into this personality then applying this strategy should stop you 'throwing your toys out of the pram' when you can't master the task straight away, and it will also encourage you to keep persevering. If you are a Perfectionist Sticker, since you won't have set yourself an impossible task, you are likely to be less stressed at not mastering the task in hand, and therefore much better at coping if you take the view that it doesn't have to be perfect immediately. You can then move onto something else, and return to this task later, knowing that you have achieved what you wanted to during this lesson.

Shy, nervous or timid

As an instructor, I deal with many pupils who are of a shy or nervous disposition. Although these pupils may potentially be good drivers, their shyness can often get in the way of their progress. If you find that you can relate to this description, then you may feel very daunted by the idea of driving lessons. Perhaps the thought of spending an hour or so in a car with a stranger fills you with dread.

I have always been quite outgoing and have a great love of cars and driving, and prior to becoming an instructor I had difficulty relating to people who were shy and had no interest in driving or cars. I didn't think that they were 'normal'. Even now, when I teach someone who is shy and nervous I see it as my goal to turn them into outgoing *Top Gear* enthusiasts.

Over the years, I have successfully managed to teach shy, nervous people to become competent drivers. At present I am teaching a young lady who had about seven or eight lessons when she was seventeen, but hated it so much, and had that horrid 'exam' feeling in her tummy before every lesson, that she discontinued taking lessons. She is now twenty-two, and has had about ten lessons with me. On the first lesson, she was very quiet and it was quite clear that she saw the lesson as an ordeal to get through. (I think that after the lesson she headed straight home for a large glass of wine to recover!) Now, when she has a lesson, we chat, have a laugh, and she has even admitted to quite enjoying it now. I am halfway towards achieving my goal with her, and the next step is for her to say to me: 'I can't wait for my next lesson'.

How to work with this personality type to your advantage

If you feel daunted by driving lessons or being in the car with a stranger, I would suggest that you talk to your instructor over the telephone, prior to your first lesson, and explain how you feel. If they are empathetic and put you at your ease you will find your first lesson much less stressful than you perhaps first anticipated. If, however, they make you feel more nervous, then perhaps a different instructor would suit you better. I always make sure that I chat to a new pupil over the telephone before their first lesson to talk through any fears that they may have, and to address any of their concerns, so that they finish the telephone call looking forwards to their lesson, rather than dreading it.

It's vitally important to have a good rapport with your instructor, especially if you are shy and nervous. You should be made to feel at ease by your instructor, and confident that he or she is there to help you. I strongly believe that your instructor should push you to a level that you can cope with, otherwise you may find yourself driving happily around at 10mph in second gear for the following six months, but this should be done in such a way that you feel relaxed and motivated. If you don't feel this way, then I urge you to find yourself an instructor that does make you feel that way.

If you haven't already done so, I suggest you take a moment at this point to look at the exercises in Chapter Five, 'Your baseline confidence'. I can't guarantee that you will turn into the life and soul of the party overnight, or suddenly want to become a Formula One racing driver, but you will find that you can work with, rather than against, your shyness by giving yourself renewed confidence. Throughout the book, you will find various visualisation and other exercises that may help you immensely.

The 'Not Bovvered' personality

If you relate to any personalities above, you will find it difficult to understand the type of person I am about to describe, as you won't be able to imagine feeling 'not bovvered' about an important skill to be mastered. However, I have taught a great many people who just don't seem bothered whether they progress quickly or slowly, if they get things right or wrong, or even appear to have any real desire to pass their test.

I was debating whether to include this personality for two reasons. Firstly, I feel that if I put one hundred percent effort into making sure I teach a good lesson, but if my pupil can't be bothered, then why should I? Secondly, I figured that people who relate to this personality type won't have felt bothered to buy this book! All instructors have pupils who appear keen, have a few lessons, then stop, then have a few more. This obviously can genuinely be down to lack of funds, having to work, lots of homework etc., but a lot of the time it's due to lack of commitment. The problem with lack of commitment is that progress can often be slow and the pupil wastes a lot of money, because when they keep starting and stopping their lessons, each time they take a lesson they find that they have forgotten so much from their previous lessons.

If I had to choose to teach someone who wasn't very good, but was prepared to give one hundred percent effort, or someone who was naturally gifted but just wasn't bothered, then I would choose the committed person every time. I think all instructors feel the same; we don't appreciate being messed about by people who aren't committed to learning.

How to work with this personality type to your advantage

If you have bought this book and do want to change this aspect of your personality, then I have some advice; think of something that you like to spend your money on; perhaps a night out with the lads/girls, clothes, holidays etc., and put a figure to this. Next, add up how much you have paid on your driving lessons so far. Is it much? Is the sacrifice of spending less money on nights out, clothes, holidays etc. for a short period equal to the amount you would save on needless extra driving lessons?

How much money do you think that you have wasted because you haven't given one hundred percent commitment to your driving lessons? Every time you have only given fifty percent commitment to your lessons, you have wasted half of your lesson cost. That means you could have passed your test in half the time, or had a few good extra nights out on the money you wasted, or put the money towards your car or insurance. You are lucky if you have so much money to waste that you can afford to do both.

I suggest that if my description above relates to you then you consider what you really want. If you really do want to learn, promise yourself and your instructor that you will give one hundred percent commitment every lesson. If you decide that you really can't be bothered to give learning to drive your all at this moment in time, do yourself and your instructor a favour, and cancel your lessons until you can feel you can commit to passing your test. If you truly want to change, try the following exercises.

Increase your motivation to learn to drive

Use the Basic Tapping Sequence for 'enhanced motivation' in Chapter One, 'How to use this book'. You may also find the sequence for 'visualisation for peak performance' useful.

Turn on your motivation

1. Think of a time when you were really motivated to do something. Remember that time now and keep running the memory through your mind as if it were yesterday. Make the image big, bold and bright. When you can remember it really well, squeeze your thumb and middle finger of either hand together.

2. Repeat this exercise several times until every time you squeeze your thumb and middle finger of your hand together you feel this same sense of motivation.

3. Keep holding your thumb and middle finger together and at the same time think about learning to drive and all the benefits you will enjoy once you have passed your test. Keep switching between the time that you have been motivated in the past and the benefits of learning to drive.

4. Repeat this exercise on a regular basis and you will soon find that you feel really motivated to persevere with learning to drive.

Learning to drive is not a game, and your instructor's car is not a toy!

This may seem like an odd description for a personality type, but nevertheless, it is very relevant. Often pupils who fit into this personality type don't treat learning to drive with the seriousness that they should do simply because they are in their instructor's car. Although your instructor is there to help you, and will certainly intervene with the dual controls if necessary, ultimately you are learning to be accountable for your actions and be aware of the responsibility you have towards your own and your passenger's safety, other road users and pedestrians, and the vehicle that you are driving. Below are two examples of how some pupils view learning to drive.

I once taught a pupil who had had about fifteen lessons. During the lesson, we approached a roundabout, and she pulled straight out without even looking, and I had to use the dual controls to prevent us from having an accident. I questioned her about how safe she had thought it was to pull out with no observation. Her answer:

'Well, it's your car; I knew that you would look, and stop the car if there was anything coming!'

One of my trainee instructors had just bought a brand new vehicle at a cost of about £13,000. On just his second day of using it for tuition, if he hadn't taken avoidance action, his pupil would have hit a kerb. The instructor talked to the pupil about the necessity of accurate steering, to avoid causing danger to other road users or pedestrians, and also several hundred pounds worth of damage to his vehicle. To the instructor's amazement, the pupil was not at all concerned with the fact that had she mounted the kerb, could have severely damaged his vehicle, and worst of all possibly injured a pedestrian. To the astonishment of my trainee instructor, she just said:

'Well, it's a tuition vehicle, it's bound to get bashed up a bit!'

Fortunately, this type of pupil is not the norm, and the majority of learners are concerned when they make a mistake that without the intervention of the instructor could have resulted in an accident. In my opinion, this is a good thing, because it teaches the value of learning to become a safe, responsible driver. However, if your reaction would have been similar to that of the pupil described above, then you need to question your attitude to driving.

How to work with this personality type to your advantage

There are two main issues to consider here. Most importantly is to ask how much value you place on someone else's life. When you are in control of a car, you are in control of a lethal weapon that has the potential to kill someone, so please consider the consequences of your actions when you are driving the car. The second issue relates to the respect that you give to your instructor's car. This may sound odd, but if you consider the pupils described above, they showed no concern or remorse that they could have injured someone, or severely damaged their instructor's vehicle. I can only assume that they would feel differently if it were their own car.

Conversely, I have often advised a pupil to speed up, and they say that they would do so if they were in their own car, but don't want to damage mine! Now, that is very considerate of them, but I advise all pupils to treat every car the same; in other words as if it were their own vehicle, and to drive it accordingly.

If you relate to any of the attributes of this personality, then please, treat learning to drive as a fun, enjoyable, pleasurable experience, but with the thought in mind of the consequences of your actions. Just remember that every time that your instructor has to take control of the steering or of the dual controls, they have prevented a potential accident that **you** would have caused. Please bear in mind that it is not your ability that is being discussed here, as you are bound to make mistakes whilst learning to drive. As a learner, your instructor doesn't expect your drive to be perfect. It's your attitude as a pupil rather than your actual driving ability that we are discussing here.

Conversation and concentration

You will know from watching other people that they are able drive whilst chatting to their passengers, listening to the radio etc. Whilst I am not suggesting that you sit in silence for the whole of your driving lesson, what you must remember is that people who feel able to do this have been driving for a long time, and driving is now as natural to them as making a cup of tea. Even so, we need to remember the great number of accidents that are caused by lack of concentration, even by experienced drivers. We need to ask why it is that smoking or the use of a mobile telephone has been banned whilst driving? The answer is obvious; these are distractions and could result in an accident, or worse still, a fatality.

Quite often, I teach pupils who appear to be more interested in telling me about their latest boyfriend or job change rather than concentrating on their driving. It's not funny when you are hurtling along a dual carriageway at 70mph in sixth gear, heading towards a roundabout, and your pupil is talking about their boyfriend/new job and they have not even spotted the roundabout. On countless occasions I have taught pupils who would, without my intervention, have sailed across junctions, roundabouts, traffic lights, and been completely oblivious to their existence. When I first started teaching pupils to drive, it used to amaze me that I had to interrupt a pupil's conversation to give them directions and instructions to enable them to deal with an upcoming junction, and that they then continued with their story as if I had been just an annoying interruption.

I do think it is important to chat with your instructor whilst on a driving lesson for several reasons. You build up a better rapport with each other, and therefore benefit more from your lessons together. In addition, once you've passed your test, realistically you're not going to sit in silence with your passengers, so learning to cope with such background activity is important. Therefore, when you are a more experienced learner and getting towards test standard, it's important to be able to carry on a conversation whilst at the same time checking your mirrors, dealing with a roundabout etc. This will prepare you for when you are out with passengers in your own car. However, there is an appropriate time for conversation, so please be guided by your instructor.

If you have ever been a passenger in a car with an experienced driver and thought that they have not noticed a hazard, you will understand how unnerving it is, to think that you may be involved in an accident because the driver is not concentrating fully.

How to work with this personality type to your advantage

Think about your last driving lesson, and ask yourself if you do have a tendency to chat at inappropriate times, or to not concentrate fully. If you relate to this description, then I ask you to take on board the following advice and guidance. You need to be aware that especially during the early lessons, you will need to concentrate fully on the physical actions required to operate the vehicle controls.

When you become more experienced, you will find that the physical ability to drive becomes almost second nature. For example, you won't have to think about the Mirror, Signal, Manoeuvre routine, or check what gear you are in, because you will be able to do these things automatically, without help from your instructor. At this time, you will be able to chat more with your instructor, but please be aware, driving requires one hundred percent concentration, one hundred percent of the time.

I'll do it properly on my test

When my partner and I were training to become driving instructors, our different personalities became very apparent. Whilst I was the perfectionist, and wanted to get everything perfect before moving onto something new, Dave's attitude was one of 'I'll fake it on the day'. Therefore, whilst I was getting more and more worked up and angry with myself when I couldn't do something properly and was concerned about reaching the required standard, Dave was calm and relaxed about the forthcoming exams. As you can imagine, this created a lot of tension between us, as we just couldn't understand each other's personalities. I couldn't understand how Dave could be so chilled when he hadn't (to my mind) practiced nearly enough, and Dave couldn't understand what I was getting so worked up about.

On many occasions, I've had to remind a pupil about something, such as feeding the steering wheel rather than just letting it spin back, or checking their mirrors, or driving with their hand on the gear lever and get the response: 'Don't worry, I won't do that on my test'. If an instructor admonishes you about something, it's for a genuine reason. In addition, I promise you that if you don't remember to do the task correctly on your lesson, you *definitely* won't remember to do it on your test, as you will be under more pressure to perform correctly. If you have read Chapter Six, 'The basics' you will know how dangerous and counter productive it is to get into bad habits; therefore I encourage you to take on board the following advice.

How to work with this personality type to your advantage

To some extent, I envy people with this type of personality. As I tend to worry about everything, to go through life not worrying, and being able to fake it seems wonderful. However, if this is your personality, it does have its' downside. It's all very well to think that you can fake it on the day and for many things, this can be true. Unfortunately though, this is not the case when it comes to driving. Everything that you do on your driving lessons prepares your for your driving test, and for safe driving for life.

One of my trainee instructors was teaching a pupil recently who just would not look in their exterior mirrors when changing lanes, or going around parked vehicles. When challenged about this, the pupil said, 'but I'll do it on my test'. I ask the question: just how dangerous is that? I can only assume that the pupil thought it was perfectly acceptable to pull out and possibly kill another motorist, just so long as they didn't do it on their driving test. Please, I urge you, for everyone's sake, drive at all times how you think you should drive when you are on your driving test, and how I hope you would expect someone else to drive if you were a passenger in their car, and they were responsible for your safety.

The pupil who says:
'Don't keep telling me, I know.'
'Let me do it on my own.'
'I was just about to do that.'

From the point of view of an instructor, this is perhaps one of the most annoying personalities. All experienced instructors tend to develop a 'sixth sense', and we just 'know' when a pupil is going to forget a mirror check, or to change gear. The instructor's dilemma is this: do we correct the pupil before they make the error, or let them make the error and then discuss afterwards what the pupil should have done? Often, we will do a mixture of both, depending on how experienced the pupil is. Sometimes, it would be dangerous to let a pupil proceed without correcting the error, such as driving around a tight corner in fourth gear when they should have changed down to second gear, but at other times, we will let the pupil make the mistake because it can be beneficial to learn from mistakes.

This personality becomes an issue when a pupil frequently makes the same error, but doesn't believe that they are doing anything wrong and that they are in control of the vehicle. Therefore, the instructor is likely to tell the pupil beforehand to prevent the mistake happening. However, this is often greeted with, 'I know, I was just going to do it, but you didn't give me the chance!' A good example of this happening in a real life situation is when the vehicle in front brakes, and the pupil doesn't react quickly enough to it. The instructor uses the dual control brake to slow the vehicle down, much to the surprise of the pupil.

Driving examiners have the same dilemma, and again, will generally not intervene until absolutely necessary in order to give the pupil the benefit of the doubt. After failing their driving test, many candidates complain that 'the examiner braked just as I was about to'. Believe me, your instructor or examiner will have given you every chance, and would have left it to the last possible moment to intervene. The point at which the instructor or examiner takes action is when they deem that it would be too late for the pupil to handle the situation themselves.

How to work with this personality type to your advantage

If you have this personality type, the good aspect is that you obviously have a lot of confidence; otherwise, you would not be questioning your instructor's judgement when they intervene. However, you must be realistic about your ability, and if you do frequently say to your instructor, 'I was just about to do that', then remember that your instructor is a much more experienced driver than you are, and you should take on board their advice. If you were 'just about to do...', then you need to be acting sooner and not leaving your actions to the last possible moment.

For example, as an instructor it's easy to spot when a pupil is going to forget their Mirror, Signal, Manoeuvre routine, because their hand will move towards the gearlever in preparation for changing gear before it moves towards the indicator in order to signal. When your instructor spots this, it's no good telling him that you were just about to signal before changing gear, as it's quite evident that you weren't.

If you find that your instructor does frequently intervene, either verbally or physically by using the dual controls, and you personally think that you were in total control and driving correctly, then discuss with your instructor what you need to do differently in order to prevent them from having to take action.

Pushy pupil or bad instruction?

This can be a difficult personality for any instructor to deal with. Fortunately, I have not had many of these pupils during my career, but when I do get one, it takes all my skills as an instructor and therapist to get a correct balance. You may be asking what do I mean by the 'pushy pupil'? A pushy pupil is the type of pupil who constantly asks the question 'when can I take my test?', usually at the same time that I'm grabbing the steering wheel to prevent them from hitting a car! This type of pupil really doesn't have a clue as to what standard of driving is actually required for the test, and more worryingly doesn't generally realise how below test standard their current driving ability is.

A few years ago, I taught a pupil who had had nearly thirty lessons with another instructor, but was recommended to me because she thought that she wasn't progressing quickly enough. When I first met her, she told me that after thirty lessons the instructor hadn't let her drive above about 40mph, hadn't done any manoeuvres and hadn't let her go on any major roads. It would have been easy for me to criticise the instructor for holding her back, but I took the view that there must have been a reason for this.

I was to find out soon enough. She wouldn't do anything off her own bat; everything had to be prompted, from putting the vehicle into gear, getting the bite, checking her mirrors, to changing gear. If I didn't instruct her to do something, then it wouldn't be done. She would have driven round in first gear for an hour if I hadn't told her to change gear.

I taught her before I trained in the techniques that I now use, and I had the same problems with her that her previous instructor had; every lesson seemed like a repetition of the last. After thirty lessons with me (that's about sixty in total) she had improved a little but every lesson I still had to tell her to do everything. On one lesson, we went down a stretch of dual carriageway, and there was a large white van parked in the left lane which she would not have noticed had I not told her how to negotiate it. This van is usually parked in the same spot, so for the following ten or so lessons, I decided to take her down the same stretch of road to see if she would either see that the van was there, or hopefully remember from the previous lesson that a vehicle may be parked there. With the majority of pupils, I would tell them the first time how to deal with a situation, with a view to prompting them the next time; something along the lines of, 'what can you see ahead, and how do you think you need to deal with it?' After this, I would hope that the pupil would be able to spot the hazard for themselves and negotiate it safely. However, with this particular pupil, even after ten or so hours, she would have just driven into the van or done an emergency stop when she saw it at the last moment if I hadn't told her to drive around it.

Every lesson, I prompted her to start some work on her theory and hazard perception as this would help with her driving lessons as well. In total she had been learning to drive for nearly eighteen months when one day she said to me: 'I really need to pass this driving test, I've been driving for ages, paid out loads of money to you, and you haven't even mentioned about me taking my test'. I was flabbergasted. I asked her what work she had been doing on her theory test, and she admitted that she hadn't even got a theory disk. I was given the very strong impression that it was my fault that she wasn't taking her test sometime soon. To make matters worse, after this particular lesson, I was met by her father who accused me of 'taking money off my daughter, and why isn't she booked in for her driving test?' You may wonder what the solution to this situation was. I invited him to sit in on her next few driving lessons.

He soon saw that I was teaching well, but that his daughter just didn't progress or act on the information that she was being given.

How to work with this personality type to your advantage

You can see how frustrating this type of pupil is to an instructor. As instructors, we have the pupil's best interests at heart and it's as demoralising for us to teach a pupil who pushes to do their test when they are not ready, as it is for the pupil who thinks that they are being held back by their instructor. The problem is how do you know if your instructor is holding you back, or if your instructor's judgement is sound? Well, you probably don't want to hear this if you are in this position, but in my experience there aren't many instructors who are just in it for the money, and the likelihood is if you instructor doesn't think you are ready for your test, then you aren't.

I do have two suggestions that you may find useful. I hope that my pupils always value my judgement and I would feel quite offended if they decided to go to another instructor for a second opinion, as I would hope that they had faith in my ability. However, if you really do feel that your instructor is holding you back, you could ask another instructor for their opinion. Think carefully of the consequences of this though. What happens if the second instructor agrees with the first? Do you stay with the first instructor and feel that you have gone behind their back? If the second instructor thinks you are ready for your test, then perhaps you would feel better swapping to this other instructor.

The second option, which I think is much better, is to ask your instructor to conduct a 'mock' test to assess how close to your test you are. If you can complete the test to a reasonable standard, then you are in a much better position to ask your instructor when you can put in for your driving test.

Whatever your personality type you can work with it to your advantage to ensure that you don't let it hinder your progress. If you take on board the advice offered, you may find that the positive aspects of your personality type are enhanced, whilst at the same time, the negative traits are diminished.

Chapter Nine

Dyslexic and dyspraxic dilemma

By Sandra Read, Certificate in Education,
OCR Diploma, SpLD, MPNLP

How to help these learners as a driving instructor and how to help yourself if you have dyslexia/dyspraxia

Throughout this chapter, you will find a great deal of very useful information written especially for learners who are dyslexic or dyspraxic. All of the technical information has been researched and written by Sandra Read, Certificate in Education/OCR Diploma SpLD/Master Practitioner NLP. Sandra has spent many years teaching in this field, and it is for this reason that I've turned to her for her specialist help and advice. If you would like to find out more, her contact details are in the Further reading and useful contacts section at the back of the book.

Thought Field Therapy can be very beneficial for anyone who is dyslexic, and has a range of techniques to reduce issues such as problems with short term memory, directionality, or sequencing. If you are dyslexic and would like more information, please contact me via the book's website www.Lofaway2pass.com or at www.tapstherapy. co.uk

Frequently, people who are dyslexic have issues with toxins. Therefore, I suggest that you take a look at Chapter Ten, 'Toxins - are they influencing your driving ability', by Sean Quigley who is an expert in this field.

Note to learner drivers

Your driving instructor will not be aware that you are dyslexic or dyspraxic unless you tell them. You need to tell them about your dyslexia and ask them to work with you using the suggestions in this chapter. I suggest you ask them if they would mind reading this chapter before your next lesson. Until I started research for this book, I just thought that people with dyslexia just 'muddled their letters up', and this is likely to be all your driving instructor knows about dyslexia (unless of course they are dyslexic themselves or know someone who is dyslexic). Unfortunately, this is often the generalised view. You may find that your instructor doesn't really understand how debilitating dyslexia can be to you when learning to drive.

If you have a good instructor, they should be willing to help you in any way that they can, and to work with you to make learning as enjoyable and easy as possible. If however, you find that your instructor is unwilling to use the suggestions in this chapter, you may want to question whether this person is the most beneficial instructor for you. Ultimately, your aim is to pass your test stress free and in fewer lessons. This chapter will help you do this; if your instructor is not willing to take on board the suggestions, then this may result in you taking longer to pass your test. The choice is yours.

Note to driving instructors

Before I started researching this book, I, like many people didn't realise how debilitating dyslexia can be for learner drivers. If you are reading this with the intention of helping your learners then I commend you. It's often difficult as instructors to accept that our standard method of teaching is not always the most appropriate and in taking on board the suggestions in this chapter, you are taking the first steps in making a difference for your dyslexic or dyspraxic learners. You may not find all the suggestions work for you and your pupils, if this is the case experiment and find what works for you.

Dyslexia and Learning—what is dyslexia?

The word 'dyslexia' comes from the Greek prefix 'dys', meaning difficulty or malfunction and root 'lexis', meaning language. There are two types of dyslexia:

Developmental Dyslexia is the name given to the condition whereby children may be born with a language dysfunction or experience some developmental delay in processing language and acquiring written language skills.

Acquired Dyslexia occurs due to damage to the brain which can be caused by cerebrovascular accident such as a head injury or a brain tumour.

Dyslexia Institute (1996)

Dyslexia is a specific learning difficulty that hinders the learning of literacy skills. This problem with managing verbal codes in memory is neurologically based and tends to run in families. Other symbolic systems, such as mathematics and musical notation can also be affected.

Dyslexia can occur at any level of intellectual ability. It can accompany, but is not a result of, lack of motivation, emotional disturbance, sensory impairment or meagre opportunities.

The effects of dyslexia can be alleviated by skilled specialist teaching and committed learning. Moreover many dyslexic people have visual and spatial abilities which enable them to be successful in a wide range of careers.

Indicators of dyslexia may include:

A problem with directionality.
A sequencing problem.
An organisational problem.
A difficulty with time.
A difficulty in motor integration.
A weakness of short-term memory.

Depending on the areas of difficulty in processing language, individuals with dyslexia will experience a range of these difficulties but not necessarily all of them (Krupska and Klein, 1995).

Incidence

Four percent of the population are severely dyslexic and up to ten percent have some degree of dyslexia (British Dyslexia Association 2001).

There is a ratio of about Three males to every one female.

Eighty-one per cent of individuals with dyslexia also have at least one close family member with the same condition (Ott 1997).

Common problems and solutions
A problem with directionality

Many learners with dyslexia and other specific learning difficulties experience confusion between left and right. This is problematical when learning to drive. If you experience this difficulty and have read previous chapters, you will have learnt about 'Psychological Reversal'. If you are Psychologically Reversed, this results in the aforementioned confusion between left and right. In order to correct this negative energy back to positive energy, all you need to do is to tap the side of either hand (where you would do a karate chop) several times. In most instances, this will ensure that you do not get left/right mixed up. In addition, you can try the following strategies.

Strategies to combat this issue

Your instructor could help you by asking you to show them left and right, before driving or manoeuvring, with your hands and by asking you to point and saying 'this is left' 'this is right' at the same time.

They could also use small coloured labels attached to the steering wheel clearly marked left and right – this simple strategy is multi-sensory and will help you to reinforce the correct directionality into your long-term memory. Your instructor should follow this up with a coloured diagram indicating left and right and reinforce this point at the beginning of every lesson.

A sequencing problem

Sequencing information in to the correct order can be very difficult for dyslexic learners. This can apply to written, verbal or pictorial information.

Strategies to combat this issue

Your instructor could give you an overview of what they are about to teach you and why for each section of the lesson. This helps to put the learning in to context and to allow the learner to assimilate the learning in a holistic way. It is best that the instructor does not give too much information verbally, rather they should break it down in to manageable 'chunks'. After presenting the information verbally, demonstrating and getting the learner to carry it out, the instructor should always back this up with a colourful diagram, numbered Mindmap (see Multi-Sensory Teaching and Learning) and brief written instructions.

You will then need to repeat back the sequence of actions required (to your instructor) to check you have them in the correct order and have understood them.

All learner drivers, whether dyslexic or not, are more likely to remember something if they understand the reason behind it. This is especially true when learning the Mirror, Signal, Position, Speed and Look routine. This very important routine forms the basis of all driving and as such all readers with dyslexia will benefit from reading Chapter Six, 'The basics' as this details why the sequence is so important.

An organisational problem/A problem with time

Difficulties with organisational skills are also linked with memory difficulties and directional difficulties, as is a lack of perception of time. They are all facets of an overall problem with processing, accessing and retaining information.

Dyslexic individuals often confuse dates and times and can have 'chaotic' personal organisation skills. However, it can often be the case that a dyslexic learner will often over compensate for these problems by being fanatically organised to the point of obsession.

Strategies to combat this issue

You might find it helpful to keep a diary of important dates, times and events to remember. Colour coded adhesive strips (available in small packs from stationers), can act as useful markers to indicate important information. Personal planners of any description with deadlines and key points to remember will help (see Multi-sensory Teaching and Learning).

A difficulty in motor integration

Visual-motor integration is the ability to discriminate accurately complex visual information and to use fine motor skills (body movements) to copy or reproduce this information. Written language skills rely on automatic integration between the auditory and visual-spatial areas of the brain and the signals arriving to the brain from the muscles and joints in the body. An individual with poor visual-motor integration skills may respond better orally than with written answers.

Strategies to combat this issue

Writing is not a skill that is needed for learning to drive but it is useful for your instructor to be aware of these difficulties when using multi-sensory teaching methods and therefore adaptations can be made to a teaching/learning programme to suit the individual.

A weakness of short-term memory

Dyslexics often have problems with short-term memory, (in other words, their 'working memory'). It can therefore take longer for dyslexic individuals to encode information for effective storage and retrieval into the long-term memory. However, once the learner gets the information into their long-term memory, it is usually secure. The problem with retrieval of this information is not stupidity or lack of cognitive skills but is usually caused by slower processing skills due to a problem with coding either the visual or phonological (sound) aspects of language or both.

Strategies to combat this issue

Using the variety of multi-sensory strategies described in Multi-Sensory Teaching and Learning will help you to absorb and retain information more efficiently.

All of the visualisation exercises throughout this book will be especially useful to you as a dyslexic learner because it will help you to transfer the 'working memory' information that you learned on your latest driving lesson, into your long-term memory, therefore enabling you to retrieve it much more easily on subsequent lessons.

Don't rely on verbal explanations – ask your instructor if it is possible for them to back up verbal explanations with a handout and hands-on demonstration and activity. In some chapters, you will find blank pages for you and your instructor to record notes to aid you to absorb the information into your long-term memory.

Your instructor needs to be aware that you need time to process information. Ask him or her to break up new learning in to small chunks with time to take information in and to ask questions, and to build in plenty of reinforcement activities and 'over learning'.

Dyslexia and self-esteem

Many dyslexics have low self-esteem because they have had extremely negative learning experiences at school. A pattern of academic failure, reinforced by negative comments on their achievements in the academic system, can create a self-defeating cycle of poor expectation about successfully completing and achieving aims that require competence and the ability to learn new skills.

Some dyslexics develop barriers to learning that contribute to their poor self worth. Your instructor is not likely to be aware of this, so they may not be as understanding as you would expect. If you are an instructor, please bear in mind that it will be necessary when working with these learners to enhance and focus on their strengths by understanding and supporting their weaknesses.

There are many successful public and historical figures who are reported to have been, or to be, dyslexic. These include:

Albert Einstein (Physicist)
Leonardo Da Vinci (Artist and Inventor)
Tom Cruise (Actor)
Susan Hampshire (Actress)
Duncan Goodhew (Swimmer)
Thomas Eddison (Inventor)
Lord Rogers (Architect)
Eddie Izzard (Entertainer)
Henry Winkler (Actor, Director, Author)

It is important for you to work towards changing the negative patterns of thinking that may have contributed to the development of low self-esteem. This can be done by using NLP and TFT techniques and using the strategies described in this chapter. If you do suffer with low self esteem and would like to build your confidence, then try Exercise Three in Chapter Thirteen, 'Test day stress-busters.' This Thought Field Therapy technique is an incredibly effective method of improving your confidence and self esteem.

In order to improve your learning experience, your instructor should always give constructive and positive feedback.

What can be done to help the dyslexic learner?

The learning process should always be a positive and active co-operation between you and your instructor. You both need to take regular time out to discuss whether or not a strategy has been successful. Focusing on your strengths will enable your instructor to provide opportunities for an immediate experience of achievement and success - essential where self-esteem is low.

Dyslexic learners often have difficulties in visual or auditory and short-term working memory and processing. Sometimes they have a combination of the two, which can be a double whammy. Whichever area of processing causes the problem, it can be bolstered by using the stronger area to aid learning or presenting information in a variety of ways which stimulates all of the learning modalities or channels.

There are a number of strategies that you can use with your instructor to help with dyslexia. The most useful strategies will empower you to use your intrinsic strengths to improve your weaknesses. This can be done by employing multi-sensory learning techniques.

Multi-sensory teaching and learning

An important note

Multi-sensory learning is not just for dyslexic individuals or those with 'difficulties'; it is a way of learning that utilises all of an individual's senses to make learning more effective and certainly more enjoyable.

Multi-sensory learning techniques are simply methods of learning which employ all of the sensory channels or modalities such as visual (sight), auditory (hearing), kinaesthetic (hands on), olfactory (smell) and even gustatory (taste).

Have you ever heard a piece of music and found that it stimulated a strong memory of events? When this happens you have triggered this memory by association with the particular song or melody. This is a strategy that can be employed for learning. Simple examples of this ability are children's learning rhymes, e.g. 'I before E except after C' to remember a spelling pattern, or songs to help remember times tables.

You can employ this skill to learn any subject including learning to drive. Together with your instructor you can tailor an individual programme to present information in a variety of ways, using all the sensory channels and working with your preferred learning styles. The most important factor of multi-sensory learning is creating the best possible environment and opportunities for you to use as many of your senses as possible in learning activities.

So, just how much do you want to pass your test in fewer repetitive lessons?

Below you will find exercises, learning styles and techniques that are remarkably effective. Some of the suggestions will take perhaps a few minutes every day, and not just during your driving lesson. A few minutes spent every day using the suggestions that follow will result in a reduction in the number of lessons that you will ultimately need to pass your driving test. Not every suggestion will work for you, so you need to experiment and use which ones you think will be of most benefit. Ask yourself: are a few minutes a day of extra effort worth it for the satisfaction of passing your test in fewer lessons?

How can this be done?

Your instructor could ask you to complete a Learning Styles Questionnaire. This would reveal your preferred learning style and be a good starting point for any learning programme.

If you prefer to learn kinaesthetically, (by doing/hands on), this will be the most successful way of teaching you any new skill. All learning goals should be structured in the most hands on way possible, but reinforced using other sensory channels.

For example you will find a demonstration, followed by you trying the new learning goal, reinforced by explanation, discussion and a very visual handout of the skill learned, using diagrams, flowcharts and mind maps very helpful.

A visual and colourful chart, using diagrams and symbols is ideal for showing progress and achievement, and you will find this a very useful tool for revision and also as a sound method for linking and structuring learning.

Always remember!

A dyslexic learner has difficulty in retaining information in their short-term memory, particularly information presented verbally. It is essential therefore for your instructor not to overwhelm you with too much information. It is also essential not to expect your learning to take place too quickly.

A dyslexic learner needs time to process and absorb information. Subjects should be linked and revised, with lots and lots of over learning to ensure retention.

Learning styles

After analysing your strengths and weaknesses to discover your preferred learning style, your instructor should use the results to develop strategies for learning. There are some excellent learning styles questionnaires available (see further reading and useful contacts section at back of book).

Multi-sensory teaching

Your instructor should encourage you to use all your senses to learn a skill – this is a very holistic approach and helps the individual to use their strengths to support their weaknesses.

On the pages that follow, you will find different multi-sensory teaching techniques. I suggest that you use the ones that you think will benefit you most.

Tactile touch

Ask your instructor to demonstrate physically movements to you, whilst at the same time talking through them. This will reinforce your learning experience. This is particularly useful when trying to learn the manoeuvres. Have a look at Chapter Seven, 'Mastering the manoeuvres' as there are visualisation exercises that will help you to learn much more quickly and to transfer this newly taught skill from your short term 'working memory' to your long term memory, making sure that you never forget them.

Sound

If your instructor is happy for you to do so, verbally describe the action that you are going to perform, such as a manoeuvre before you carry out the action during your lessons. Explain to your instructor that this will help you to remember it more easily. It may be helpful to record this onto a tape (a small hand held Dictaphone is ideal for doing this, and not expensive) and then play it back after your lesson, write it down, perhaps in short bullet points. You can then use this to revise during the time before your next lesson. If your instructor is reluctant to let you do this, perhaps saying that it will take too long, then remind them that it will take them longer the next lesson to repeat everything that they have just taught you on this lesson.

The use of music is sometimes beneficial – to aid relaxation and memory – here you can be creative. Research suggests that listening to Baroque style music whilst revising aids memory and learning. The rhythm and patterns contained in this type of music apparently aid the learning process.

This is perhaps the most controversial request that you will make of your instructor. Most instructors would find this request odd, as logically it would seem that this would take your concentration away from listening to their instructions. If you genuinely think that music played on your instructor's car's CD player (quietly of course, just as 'background noise') is going to help you, explain the reason behind it, and ask your instructor if they are prepared to give it a try. You may have to provide the CD though; perhaps the instructor's *Bat out of Hell* Meatloaf CD may not be the most useful learning aid! Although, for all Meatloaf fans out there, his songs are suited to learning to drive with lines like: 'Objects in the rear view mirror may appear closer than they are', and: 'I didn't see the sudden curve until way too late'!

Sight

It will be beneficial to you if you and your instructor use colour coding and highlighter pens for individual written notes and instructions, such as handouts and cards. You could ask your instructor if each lesson could be summarised on to a card using bullet points on one side and diagrams on the other (see Memory Trees). Written instructions could be represented by symbols, to aid retention in to long-term memory.

Taste and smell

Some learners may find it useful to have a smell introduced - lavender oil, incense etc. to associate a new learning point with a scent: this can sometimes aid memory. For example each different smell (perhaps using a variety of essential oils) could be introduced with each new topic, such as reversing around a corner.

Your instructor may find this request rather unorthodox and respond as if you have taken leave of your senses! This is why I encourage you to show this chapter to your instructor before adopting any of these techniques. Your 'senses' are exactly what we are talking about here; how 'Multi-Sensory Learning' can be tailored to each individual's needs. This may seem like an odd request, and may be met with objections from your instructor because other pupils after you may object to strong smells left over from your lesson! However, there is also research that shows that it is helpful to chew gum or suck peppermints as an aid to memory, as this raises alertness by changing brainwaves. This may be of benefit to you, and this is less likely to create an issue for your driving instructor.

However, although the introduction of tastes/smells may be an aid to learning, frequently these items can be toxic to an individual. Therefore, I suggest that you read Chapter Ten, 'Toxins – are they influencing your driving ability?' as in some circumstances, they may prove more detrimental than beneficial. Unless your preferred learning style really does benefit from the introduction of tastes or smells, then I would suggest that you make more use of the other senses as described above, to avoid the possibility of toxins having a detrimental influence on your driving.

Writing

You may also find it beneficial to write key words or instructions down whilst saying them at the same time, then to read them back (silently to yourself if you are self-conscious about reading aloud). Another useful tip is to write these key words or instructions onto small post-it notes and to put them in prominent places, so that you are reminded of them on a regular basis between your driving lessons.

Cloze exercises

These could be based on the driving lesson just completed and done as revision homework. They consist of homemade written passages that are tailored to the concepts or learning points that the you are working on. Your instructor can use an appropriate level of text and leave spaces for you to insert the words in the correct places. For instance, the sequence of actions in a Hill Start. This activity reinforces skills practised and learned and continues the multi-sensory theme. There is a section at the end of Chapter Six, 'The basics' for you/your instructor to write notes. You could use this section to try this exercise.

Teaching rules

Guidelines for instructors using these techniques

Your instructor should always teach at a rate that suits your needs: one a week is probably realistic, after a practical session. You shouldn't overload yourself! Your instructor should always use multi-sensory methods to do this and only concentrate on one new point at a time.

Mnemonics – memory joggers

You can use colour, rhyme, post-it notes, highlighter pens and a sense of humour to create memory joggers for easily remembering learning points. For instance: Sequences of actions for performing manoeuvres, using mirrors, or interpreting road signs.

Revise frequently!

Your instructor should never assume that a dyslexic learner 'knows' a fact or learning point after one success. Therefore, your instructor should regularly revisit the concept so that you can complete it confidently on at least three consecutive occasions. It's important that your instructor builds regular practice of what you have been working on into the teaching programme. For example, if you have practiced a turn in the road on one lesson, make sure that you get to practice it on the next few lessons, rather than not doing it again until a few lessons later. I know that this may be difficult as often an instructor will have a 'lesson plan' in mind, but if they are aware of which method of learning is more beneficial to you, then a good instructor will do their utmost to help you to learn by this method. The key to success is small, linked, structured multi-sensory steps, to be reviewed at each stage.

Memory trees

You can use Memory Trees to help remember any important information, prior to a test or just for revision. Use a separate card to summarise each topic. Then summarise all of the topics on to one card prior to a test. You could have text in bullet points on one side of the card and a picture or diagram on the other, to aid memory. You should use lots of colour. Summarise each topic on to a card. Summarise each card on to one final card.

Mindmapping and accelerated learning

This is a technique used to plan or remember a series of connected ideas/actions/learning points. It can incorporate all of the multi-sensory strategies mentioned previously in this chapter, such as colour, visual images and writing.

Mindmapping is:

Using memory trees to revise previously learned points. Putting yourself in to a positive state - prior to lessons and tests (see NLP, TFT and Brain Gym).

Using visualisation techniques, such as those described in Multi-sensory Learning or the section on NLP Techniques.

Taking regular breaks when learning new things - fall back and don't overload!

Use Mindmaps to:

Help remember previous lessons and new techniques.

Plan the sequence of manoeuvres (you could number them if this helps).

Remember instructions.

Reinforce memory and link ideas and movements.

Dyslexic learners and visual disturbance/ instability syndrome

Many individuals with dyslexia have extreme difficulty in reading black text on a white background. This difficulty is sometimes known as `Irlen Syndrome'. There are a variety of possible causes for this problem, but it is exacerbated by the bleaching process used in the production of white paper. Reading can be greatly assisted by the use of pastel coloured paper for all reading materials and by using an alternative font colour to black for the text. Handouts and written materials should always be in at least a size 12 font and it is much easier for learners with dyslexia to read rounded and well spaced fonts, such as Arial and Comic Sans. Times Roman is not a good choice.

Coloured overlays/reading rulers

When researching for this book, we discussed the possibility of printing on coloured paper, but unfortunately this was not a viable proposition due to printing costs. However, there are a number of companies that provide coloured acetate overlays and reading rulers to help with visual instability. These overlays can have a dramatic impact on reading speed and the ability to 'keep your place' when reading.

You may find it useful to have a test for visual instability carried out by a qualified dyslexia specialist to determine which colours would be most suitable. Please see the resources/contacts page at the back of the book for more information about these products and where to get them.

Some individuals with visual disturbance benefit from wearing tinted spectacles. A vision test can be carried out by a specialist optometrist who will be able to advise on the most appropriate colour.

Dyspraxia and learning to drive

In many ways dyslexia and dyspraxia are similar. It is also possible for the same person to have both. Dyslexia is primarily a difficulty with language and impacts on learning to write, to read and to spell. Individuals with dyslexia sometimes have other problems such as poor organisational skills.

Dyspraxia is mainly an impairment of the organisation of movement such as hand/eye or other forms of co-ordination, but it can also affect skills involved in language, thought and perception.

Problems associated with dyspraxia

Planning movements and being aware of the space around them: Dyspraxic individuals are often perceived as 'clumsy'.

Perception: dyspraxic individuals can experience difficulty in judging heights and distances, which may cause issues when learning to drive with such things as passing obstacles such as parked cars, or cyclists, and manoeuvres such as judging the distance from the kerb or the white lines in a parking bay.

Co-ordination: dyspraxic individuals find it difficult to move parts of the body without looking and also to move in sequence. When driving this often causes problems such as steering whilst changing gear, and without looking at the gear lever. You will find more helpful information to help alleviate these issues in Chapter Six, 'The basics'.

Laterality: working out left from right without a reminder. This is a problem whilst driving, especially when you are heading towards a junction and not knowing which way you are meant to be going. At the start of this chapter, you will find a simple technique to help you to work out which way is left and which way is right.

Concentration: dyspraxic individuals may need longer to complete a task and find it very difficult to 'multitask'.

Short-term memory and sequencing tasks: it can be difficult to make sense of information when listening or reading instructions, taking notes and dealing with maps and charts. Forgetting and losing things can be a major problem.

Organisation: those with dyspraxia often have little sense of direction or time. They also find it difficult to organise themselves and their work and can sometimes find it hard to express themselves.

Because of these difficulties, individuals with dyspraxia can easily become depressed, frustrated and disheartened. Many have low self-esteem. These individuals are also very prone to 'good' and 'bad' days.

Strategies for those working with dyspraxic learners

Any of the strategies described in the section on dyslexia will benefit you if you have dyspraxia.

Your instructor needs to show understanding and empathy, this is essential: repetition, revision and 'over learning' are vital.

As with dyslexia using multi-sensory techniques to learn new skills is essential. Your instructor should spend time describing, demonstrating, asking you to verbalise back. They should also ask open questions to check understanding and provide handouts with colourful diagrams and flow-charts, accompanied by clear written instructions. All these things will help.

Together with your instructor you could use colour coded stickers with Left/Right on the steering wheel to indicate direction. The instructor could try asking you to say 'I am turning right' or 'I am indicating left' at the same time as performing the action as this may help to improve orientation when following directions.

You will find that training in relaxation techniques, confidence building and related strategies such as those described in the NLP, Brain Gym and Thought Field Therapy sections will be beneficial to you.

You could try learning strategies to compensate for weak memory and organisational skills. Making use of organisers such as daily/weekly planners and other timetables is especially beneficial. You could also use Mindmaps to organise new learning points or skills to practise.

You might want to try using a Dictaphone (hand held tape recorder) to enable you to record important learning points and play them back to revise. There are digital models available that can download information to a PC. If you also have a programme such as Read and Write (Texthelp) on your PC, the information can then be read back to you, aiding concentration and understanding. This is also 'multisensory'.

Brain gym to help learning
What is brain gym?

Brain Gym consists of a system of exercises which fully integrate the mind and body in readiness for learning. It has been used with children and adults and can be especially beneficial for learners with dyspraxia and dyslexia. The following are examples of the steps to follow to achieve this:

It is especially helpful for people who have any learning difficulty or anyone in a learning situation, to drink plenty of water. Water increases the oxygen uptake and helps to increase the speed of communication in the central nervous system. I suggest that you always drink water before a lesson or test and throughout the day (at least six glasses).

Using the thumb and forefinger to stimulate gently the area just below the collar bone, in a circular movement, is an aid to concentration. This stimulates the carotid artery which carries blood to the brain, helping to promote thinking and learning processes. You could try to do this before/during each lesson.

Standing up and 'cross crawl' is another method you can adopt to aid your learning. You need to raise your knee and alternate arm so that they meet. Continue this for a few minutes. This exercise will help you to integrate the communication between the left and right sides of the brain, making learning easier.

continued...

You may find that sitting comfortably and crossing your feet at the ankles is beneficial to learning (though do not do the latter part during your lessons!). You need to place the hands together as though praying. Then turn your hands over so that the palms of both hands are facing one another then let your fingers slide through each other to link up. Turn your hands under and rest them on your breast bone. This exercise will help to calm and relax your mind and prepare it for the challenges of learning or for a test situation.

Using NLP to help learning
The happiness and relaxation trigger

1. Close your eyes and remember a time when you felt wonderfully happy and excited. See what you saw, feel what you felt, hear what you heard. Look at the picture of this memory in your mind and notice:

2. Is it a still photograph or a movie? If it is a still photograph see if you can change it to a movie.

3. Is it in colour or black and white? If it is in black and white see if you can change it to colour and make the colours as bright and bold as possible. Make the picture as big and vivid as you can.

4. Can you smell anything? Try to remember any smells that were associated with this memory.

6. If there are any sounds such as music – listen to them and let them wash over you again, stimulating the memory.

7. Let the strong feelings you had flow through you and see if you can intensify them. When the feelings are as wonderful as you can possibly recall them, move onto step 8.

8. Press together your thumb and your middle finger to 'anchor' this feeling. Do this several times when you are feeling most happy in your memory.

9. As you continue to look at the picture/movie – float in to it so that you are a part of it – look around you and make it even more vivid.

10. 'Anchor' this feeling again.

The success trigger

For this exercise close your eyes and remember a time when you were learning something and you learned it easily and brilliantly. It doesn't matter what the 'something' was - it could be knitting, bricklaying, nuclear physics or history. The important thing is that learning this skill/subject made you feel happy and successful.

Recall the satisfaction and curiosity you felt when you were going through this learning process successfully - each step taking you nearer to achieving your goal. See what you saw, feel what you felt, hear what you heard. Look at the picture of this memory in your mind and notice the way it makes you feel

Repeat steps 1-8 of The Happiness Trigger

Before a driving lesson or test take some time in a quiet place to:

Visualise your happy self and step in to it.
Visualise your successful learning self and step in to it.
Power up your positive memories by using your 'anchors'. Any time you feel your confidence slip - use the anchor again - you will find that you immediately feel relaxed, happy and ready to succeed!

How to increase self-belief and raise self-esteem in what you want to achieve using the 'Swish Pattern'

You can use this powerful technique to improve confidence in any area – this example relates to driving.

Visualise the self-doubting 'you'. Make this image large and bright and colourful and place to one side for a moment.

Imagine what you would look and feel and sound like if you had achieved your goal in passing your driving test. Make this image as believable as possible. Make it big, bright, colourful and a 'movie' image if possible. While you are looking at this image add a voice to it which tells you how important this is to you and how much you want it.

Take the first 'negative' self-doubting image and place a small dark image of the 'successfully passed' image in the lower left hand corner of this. Make the 'negative' image go suddenly dark at the same time as the small 'successfully passed' image springs up in size, covering and replacing it. This image should be very big and bright.

Do this process very quickly at least five times in a row, making the 'swish' sound every time. Each time you do it open your eyes for a second.

How to change a bad feeling into a really good one

This technique can be used for occasions when anxiety and nerves start to take over. Close your eyes, concentrate on the bad feeling and let it wash through you.

Notice where the feeling is and in what direction it is moving. Visualise yourself pulling this feeling outside of your body and actually make the actions with your hand.

Allow the feeling to move in it's original direction for a moment.

Now take hold of the feeling and start to turn it in the opposite direction, using your hand and actually making the movements.

Spin the feeling faster and faster in the opposite direction to the one it was moving in – notice as you spin it faster and faster that the feeling changes from a bad one to a good one.

Keep spinning the feeling until you achieve an overwhelming feeling of happiness and calm.

Imagine the feeling is saturated in your favourite colour.

Push the still spinning feeling back inside your body and let it carry on spinning from the tips of your toes to the top of your head, releasing waves of colour.

When this wonderful feeling reaches its height – let it explode out of the top of your head!

Notice how incredibly relaxed and peaceful you feel and ready to take on anything!

Using timelines to program yourself for success

Timelines are a form of NLP exercise that can be used to remove negative feelings from the past and to program positive feelings in to the future. Try this exercise to set your future goals for driving success.

NB: It may help to get a sympathetic person to help you with the instructions and to talk you through them. Don't worry if you need to practise this - keep going until you have it as you want it.

Visualise your life as a line stretching into your past, through your present and in to your future as a straight 'Timeline'. Your past will be behind you and the present will usually pass through you. The future will be in front of you.

Relax and imagine your Timeline stretching out in to the future (you need to set the actual amount of time - e.g. three months, six months etc. - whatever is realistic for you), to a time when you have passed your driving test.

Notice where that position is in front of you.

Point to that point - the point where you have passed your test.

Visualise a picture of yourself, when you have passed your driving test and feel what you will feel, see what you will see and hear what you will hear when you visualise that successful picture.

Increase these feelings and the brightness of the image until you really want it and desire it.

continued...

Now take that image and move it over your timeline and place it at a point slightly further than you imagine it will be in the future. Next, move it closer to a place where it feels just right and you are certain it will happen. Bring back all of the feelings, sounds and pictures you saw in step 5 then 'anchor' this feeling by pressing together your thumb and forefinger.

Take this image out further in to the future, place yourself on this point on the timeline and look back from the future along the timeline to the present. Look at all the positive benefits you have achieved by passing your driving test and what they have meant to you. 'Anchor' these feelings as above.

Bring the image back to now (the present) and 'anchor' the positive feelings again. Then take the image in to the past and experience the thing that you have achieved as a past event. It is now something that you have already done!

Bring the image up to the present and into now. Then let it move to a place that feels and looks right. Ask yourself where this image has settled. Look at that point and visualise again the amazing feelings of successfully achieving this goal. Is it already possible or definite in the near future?

Timeline 2

You can also reinforce the first exercise by carrying out the first seven steps and then:

Stand on your present on your Timeline then slowly walk forward to the point where you have passed your driving test. You are now in the future.

Turn around and look back through the lessons and steps that successfully enabled you to achieve this.

Slowly walk back through them, visualising, feeling and seeing them one by one and feeling the feelings of achievement at each stage. 'Anchor' them one by one.

When you get back to the present look forward again to the future successful you and bring back the image, knowing that you have achieved all of the steps you need to meet this reality, in your future.

These exercises may take some practise, but they are wonderfully empowering. Try reading the instructions on to tape and playing them back to yourself if you have difficulty with retaining them.

Chapter Ten

Toxins - are they influencing your driving?

By Sean Quigley, TFT-VT, MPNLP, Cert.E.H.

As a driving instructor, I constantly deal with pupils who suffer from anxiety, nerves, lack of confidence and issues with coordination. Throughout this book, you have learned about Psychological Reversal and how to ensure that you stay in 'Positive Polarity', along with methods and techniques that will enable you to eradicate these issues. However, people are often affected by toxins which may result in an inability to rid themselves of these issues. Therefore, I have asked a leading expert on the subject, Sean Quigley, to give some help and advice on the subject of toxins. Sean is the most highly qualified Thought Field Therapist in the country and has many years experience dealing with top sports personalities, helping them to achieve success in their chosen field. You will find his contact details in the section 'Further reading and contacts' at the back of the book.

What is a toxin?

Toxins can and do affect all of us at some times in our daily life; the important point here is, what are they and how are they affecting us?

Absolutely everything can be toxic. Water if drunk to excess is toxic, even if it is pure. Toxins are not allergens; an allergen is a substance inhaled, ingested, or that you come in contact with, that causes a measurable reaction in the blood stream. These reactions can be severe and life threatening, as in the case of anaphylactic shock; or mild, with symptoms such as bloating, coughing or skin blemishes. When an item is an allergen it will normally cause an immediate reaction. There are many well known toxins that are toxic to everyone, and we usually refer to these as 'poisons' and they include arsenic, mercury, and lead.

What we are talking about in this chapter are Individual Energy Toxins (IETs). Although (IETs) can cause some of these mild reactions, they are typically substances, primarily inhaled, ingested or absorbed through the skin, such as with hair dye, creams and perfumes, that cause a negative reaction at an energy level. Many of these items are found in everyday life and are not a problem to most people; however they are still classed as an Individual Energy Toxin (IET). In short that means you or I may have specific negative reactions to anything we eat, drink, smell or are exposed to.

Most (IET) toxins can be successfully treated very quickly and after a minimum three-month period you can normally return to those foods in moderation and not have a reaction. Inhaled toxins always need to be avoided at all times and contact toxins (creams and potions etc found to be toxic) always need to be checked before re-using.

The finest quality foods, organic or otherwise, full of vitamins and minerals, may in fact be very toxic to you or me. Unfortunately it is not obvious when a food or substance is toxic; however if you pay close attention to your body and how you feel, you will almost always notice reduced energy levels and general malaise, and you may also feel increased levels of anxiety, ranging from slightly anxious to full blown panic attacks. Testing for toxins requires a high level of skill and it is always advisable to have suspected IETs and or the symptoms diagnosed by a professional.

How do I know that I'm being affected by Individual Energy Toxins?

We are all affected in varying degrees and these effects only become noticeable when we are feeling worse than our normal state. For instance we may be feeling anxious or in pain, experiencing loss of confidence and or coordination, feeling emotional or depressed, angry and frustrated, especially when we have no obvious reason to be feeling that way. If you are already experiencing some of these symptoms prior to exposure to a toxin or toxins, in general they will get even worse.

Many people often put these feelings down to an upcoming or past stressful event, never connecting the change or increase in emotional levels to something they have eaten or drunk etc.

Toxins may also make us tired and rob us of our energy and vitality; our happy-go-lucky mood may suddenly stop, so much so that we may need to have a sleep when we come in from work, or an afternoon nap for no apparent reason. Sudden tiredness and mood swings can come on at any time.

For example I once treated a world-class swimmer who was under performing following a recent move away from his home. He couldn't understand how that was affecting his performance so much; after talking to him, I discovered that he had changed his diet and was now eating a lot of pizza and pasta, which is a recognised good source of carbohydrates for sports people. I tested him to see if wheat was an IET, and it proved to be highly toxic to him. He removed wheat from his diet and within a week, improved on his best ever sprint time by half a second, a very substantial improvement for a sprint swimmer. He also reported increased energy levels generally.

So, how does this affect my driving and passing my test?

You may be wondering how, does all this relate to me? How does this affect my driving and passing my driving test? Let me explain; the side effects of toxins include Psychological Reversal (PR), anxiety, loss of concentration, tiredness,

depression, Obsessive Compulsive Disorder (OCD), Attention
Deficit Hyperactivity Disorder (ADHD), anger, road rage,
blurry vision, aches and pains, dyslexia, memory loss and
lack of coordination. Even this is not an exhaustive list
of the effects of toxins; we must also appreciate that
individuals may be affected in varying degrees, dependent
on the number and the levels of these toxins present in our
bodies at any one time.

Once we reach our own individual toxin limit or threshold,
i.e. the level of that toxic substance our bodies can safely
deal with at any one time, we can experience one or more
of the above symptoms, either emotionally or physically.
The more toxins you have in the body, the more negative
effects you will experience. Also the negative effects of
just one major toxin in our bodies may cause other foods,
drinks and / or other substances to also become more
toxic to us, thereby increasing our overall level of toxins.
These additional toxins would have normally been ok and
we would have had no negative reactions to them, but our
lymphatic system is now overloaded and cannot deal with
any more slightly toxic substances, hence the multiplying
negative effects on our bodies and minds.

Our bodies and our minds are capable of amazing things,
but, we need to understand that there are limits to our
toxin clearing abilities. Our blood has a heart pumping
approximately eight pints of blood around our bodies and
the liver and kidneys cleansing our blood. However, we
have approximately four times that volume in lymphatic
fluid and no pumps to circulate it. Activity and exercise
is the best way to promote lymphatic circulation, and
being sedentary is extremely bad for us. When we are
first learning to drive it can be a time of great stress, this
is when we are at our most vulnerable to the effects of
toxins. When we also add the stress of the driving test, we
then have even higher levels of stress. When the body is
physically or emotionally under stress and we then inhale,

contact or ingest IETs, it can have drastically negative effects on how we feel, how we process information and perform even simple tasks. To make matters worse, we are so sedentary when driving we are inhibiting our lymphatic circulation and therefore our ability to clear the toxins.

I have treated a number of clients who are anxious about driving, some of whom are anxious even when they are not in the car and are just thinking about it, and others whose problems only occur when they are actually driving. In most cases, the problem has been exacerbated by the fact that they all had air fresheners in their homes and in their cars, which are known to be highly toxic.

The plastics of car interiors and the chemicals they are cleaned or treated with, can also be toxic, and as a car is such an enclosed environment, this can cause even more problems. Combined with in-car air fresheners, this can be a recipe for disaster. The inhaled fumes become very toxic because our bodies are not getting enough clean air to dilute the effects of the air freshener or other fumes. When you reach this level of toxicity, any personal problems or concerns can become magnified to the point of extreme anxiety, you go into Psychological Reversal (PR) and may as a result struggle to perform even simple tasks.

What can I do to 'rid' myself of toxins?

Diagnosis of toxin problems is carried out by a trained TFT Dx (Diagnostic) or more accurately by VT (Voice Technology) trained Thought Field Therapist either in person (Dx) or over the phone (VT) using a highly-skilled system of vocal analysis.

Diagnosis and Treatment takes only minutes and the subsequent and ongoing removal of those diagnosed toxins from the body, for a minimum of three months, can completely eliminate the symptoms. After a retest you may make a moderate return to the foods and or drinks; however I recommend that any other type of toxin, i.e. powders, potions and lotions etc, be avoided for good, as non-toxic equivalents can almost always be found to replace them.

Psychological Reversal (PR) may or may not be connected to toxins. We can find for example that when something annoys us or we have any form of negative emotional response, we immediately become Psychologically Reversed; things can then go from bad to worse. For example, imagine a situation when you think you have made a driving mistake, have become annoyed and then done the same thing again; does this sound familiar? What if you did not make a mistake according to the examiner, or the mistake was so minor it would not have affected the outcome of your test, but due to PR you believed that you were going to fail and as a result of that belief, really did make a major mistake that subsequently lead to failure? All this can happen as a result of being in PR. If excess toxins are present then invariably you will be in PR until they are cleared.

By learning and using all of the techniques in this book and in having a good understanding of the possible effects of toxins and PR on your physical and emotional state, and how to correct PR, you are maximizing your chance of becoming a safe competent driver who can pass their test confidently first time.

Chapter Eleven

When do you want to
pass your test?

And why do you want to
pass your test?

I will return to the 'And why do you want to pass your test?' later, but firstly, I want to have a look at the question of when you want to take your test. Regardless of whether you have started taking lessons or how many you have had, ask yourself this question:

Have you set a date by which you want to have passed your test?

If the answer is no, then I want you to ask yourself why not? Obviously, it would be silly to say that you want to have passed your test by a week on Wednesday when you haven't even sat behind the wheel yet, but it is sensible to set yourself a 'pass date'. If you have already taken some lessons, then your instructor will be able to give you an estimate of how many lessons he or she thinks that you will need. Then, guided by their expertise, you can set a goal date to take your driving test.

Until your test date is looming, it's easy to put less effort into your lessons because you may find yourself thinking: 'I've got ages yet'. However, if you go to each lesson with a date in mind, then you are more likely to focus on **every** lesson, and not just the ones leading up to your test. This is also why it's also important that you and your instructor have a progress record so you can check that you are on target for the test. A test date is not set in stone, and may be altered, but if you set a date, you are at least giving yourself something to 'aim' for. A couple of sayings come to mind here: 'If you don't know where you are going, all roads lead there', and: 'If you aim for nothing, you'll hit it!' Both of these sayings are very accurate if you have not set yourself the goal of when you want to take your driving test.

And why do you want to pass your test?

You may think that this is a stupid question and that the answer is obvious. It is: to have freedom, to be able to get to work and go out with your friends, to be able to go on holidays etc. However, your motivation for taking your test is the key factor here. A good way of looking at the word 'motivation' is to look at your 'motive for action'. Ask yourself what motivates you to pass your test? If you feel that you are lacking in motivation, try the **Basic Tapping Sequence** for 'enhanced motivation' in Chapter One, 'How to use this book'. There are different types of motivation, and some types of motivation can be more powerful and beneficial to you than others. Next I want to look at 'towards' motivation and 'away' motivation.

Towards motivation

As the title suggests, this describes a situation when you are motivated towards your goal, rather like the donkey trying to get to the carrot. You really want to pass your test because it will mean a lot to you; it means that you will have your freedom. This type of motivation is good, because it is positive, and keeps you focused on your goal in a pleasurable way. You can picture yourself passing, and feel excited about it. No effort is too much trouble and you enjoy working towards it.

Away motivation

This type of motivation may be detrimental because it is negative. Rather than being motivated towards an exciting goal, you are motivated to move away from something that doesn't bring you pleasure. This is like the donkey trying to get away from the stick, or moving away from the fire in order not to be burnt. A good example of this would be if you had to pass your test by a certain date, otherwise you would not get to keep that job that requires you to drive, or struggle in your new life at university without a car.

This type of motivation is very demoralising as it puts you under immense pressure to perform, and of course, when you are under pressure, you tend to panic and things go wrong. It's much better to focus on the positive aspects of taking your driving test rather than the negative.

You may already know that you brain doesn't think in negatives, therefore in order to think of something negative, you have to think of the positive first. The usual example quoted is to 'not think of pink elephants'; up until this point the thought of a pink elephant had not even crossed your mind, but now you are thinking about it, and it's very hard not to. Away motivation is the opposite of towards motivation, and because it's negative, you have to think of the thing you want to move away from in order to not think of it. Are you confused now? I will make it simple:

I need to pass my driving test otherwise I will lose my job because my employer wants me to do deliveries; therefore I have to think about losing my job every lesson to focus on my away motivated goal!

This is very demoralising; to have to focus on the negative in order to think of your goal. Away motivation can be very depressing as you can now see. If you are in this situation, for example if you do have to pass your test by a certain date in order to keep your job, then you will not help yourself at all by continually focusing on it. If you keep thinking of all the consequences if you fail, then it will become a self-fulfilling prophecy and you are much more likely to fail. Therefore, to stop this happening you need to change your view of the situation to a positive, towards motivation.

I suggest you now work through the exercises in Chapter Twelve, 'Are you talking yourself into failure?'. Whether you use towards or away motivation is up to you, but you are much more likely to be successful on your test day if you turn away motivation into towards motivation. As a result, you will have much more confidence in your ability, feel less stressed, and find yourself focusing on something pleasurable, rather than trying to focus away from something horrid.

Chapter Twelve

Are you talking yourself into failure?

A few days before her test, Jane said to me, 'I'm really excited about my test, because if I pass I can take my daughter to the hairdressers on Thursday, and I'll be so proud of myself'. I was really pleased to hear this, as Jane was not known for her confidence. However, she immediately followed it up with, 'but I know that I'll fail because I'm absolutely useless and know that I'll never pass.' In one small sentence, she had managed to successfully talk herself into failure. This is what's known as a 'self-fulfilling prophecy'. If you keep telling yourself often enough that you can't do something, then you won't be able to do it. So often, we talk to ourselves in a negative way that we simply wouldn't accept from someone else.

During lessons, I have heard pupils call themselves stupid, thick or useless, and tell me that they will never pass their driving test. How would you feel if your driving instructor spoke to you like that? How would you react if your instructor said to you:

'You are the worst pupil that I've ever taught.
Why are you even bothering learning to drive?
The chances of you passing your test are so
remote that it's going to cost you a fortune
in lessons and failed tests.
If I were you, I'd give up now.'?

If I spoke to my pupils in this manner, I'd expect to spend the rest of the day in the Accident and Emergency department of my local hospital! The question is, if you wouldn't accept someone else talking to you like that, why do you accept it from yourself?

Do you consider yourself to have a negative or positive outlook?

The mind is neither positive nor negative by nature; it's only as 'positive' or 'negative' as you make it. Two people may drive to exactly the same standard, but their individual viewpoint of the lesson may be entirely different, depending on whether they tend to have a positive or negative outlook. For example, a pupil may stall the car five times during their lesson. (I have chosen stalling as an example, as so many pupils tend to use this as a measure of their driving ability.) When discussing the lesson, a pupil with a negative approach may say, 'that was really dreadful, I kept stalling'.

On the other hand, a pupil with a more positive outlook may say, 'It was a brilliant lesson, I only stalled a few times', and be very pleased that they drove well for fifty-five out of sixty minutes. The above description is of the exact same lesson, but shows two very different perspectives. Now, which perspective do you think is going to be psychologically of most benefit to you?

Try the following exercise to ascertain whether your thoughts regarding your driving are positive or negative.

Do you visualise your driving as positive or negative?

1. Close your eyes and think about your next driving lesson.

2. On a scale of 1-10, where 1 is easy to imagine and 10 is difficult, how easy/difficult is it for you to imagine yourself making loads of mistakes and driving badly?

3. Using the same 1-10 scale, how easy/difficult is it to imagine yourself driving really well, and being very pleased with your progress?

If you found it easier to imagine yourself driving badly, then the exercise further on in this chapter will help you to visualise yourself performing at the peak of your ability. Even if you can picture yourself driving well, I recommend that you still do the exercise, as you will be amazed at how much this visualisation exercise helps you in reality on your next lesson.

The following story is a good example of how effective visualisation can prove to be. A man went on holiday to Switzerland, and decided to learn to ski. He was lacking in both confidence and competence, and by the end of the holiday, he had not shown much improvement at all. However, the following year he returned and saw the same ski instructor. He amazed the instructor with his polished performance and the instructor asked him how many lessons he had taken during the past year. 'None', the man replied, 'but everyday, I imagined that I was you skiing down this very slope until I could do it as well as you'.

The brain learns by two processes; copying or 'modelling' how others perform a task, and then repeatedly practicing the new skill. Imagining yourself performing a skill can be as powerful as actually performing it physically. This is achieved with the power of your imagination. Therefore, when you imagine something going wrong, you are sending messages to your unconscious mind that this is what you want to happen, and you are 'helping' yourself learn how not to do it.

For example, during your lesson have you ever said something like: 'I hate hill starts, I always panic and then stall or roll back when there's a car behind me.' The reason that you stall or roll back may be that you don't have very good clutch control. However, have you ever considered that when there's nothing behind you, you are perfectly capable of starting off on a really steep hill, but as soon as there's a car behind you, you find it difficult starting off on a gentle uphill slope without panicking and then rolling back or stalling?

Remember, your physical ability to perform a hill start doesn't suddenly leave you when there is a car behind you.

So what changes? The answer is simple: your confidence in your ability. As soon as there is a car behind you, all sorts of negative thoughts may come into your head. It's these negative thoughts that prevent you from doing a good hill start, because you tell yourself that you are going to roll back or stall, even though you know that you are capable of good clutch control. The technique to perform a hill start is **exactly** the same regardless of whether there is a car behind you or not.

The question is: what can you do about it? Assuming that you are 'physically' capable of hill starts, the following exercises will ensure that you have the 'mental' ability to perform them correctly **every time without fail** whether there are cars behind you or not. I use hill starts as an example, as this is a skill that many pupils worry about, but you can substitute any problem area that you may have a 'mental block' with, for example, large roundabouts with lots of lanes and exits, manoeuvres, or dual carriageways etc. All of these exercises are effective on their own, but even more so if you practice them all. You just have to tailor them to suit your individual needs.

Exercise One
Test yourself for 'Specific Reversal'

This exercise is designed to help you combat any negative feelings and emotions that you have towards specific problem areas. If you have read Chapter, Five 'Your baseline confidence level', you may already be familiar with this exercise, which was used to test if you were reversed to learning to drive with confidence. I hope that you have followed my advice in this chapter; tapping the side of your hand on a regular basis to ensure that you are in positive polarity. However, although you should now feel confident with your general driving, you may be 'Psychologically Reversed' in one particular 'problem area' such as those described above. Therefore, I suggest that you follow the exercise described in Chapter Five 'Your baseline confidence level', but replace the statements with the issues that are pertinent to you, such as in the example shown below.

Statement	Strong arm	Weak arm
* I want to perform hill Starts with confidence	You genuinely want to perform hill starts with confidence and are likely to be successful	On a deeper level, you do not want to perform hill starts with confidence and will sabotage your own attempts to learn to drive with confidence. Use the corrective treatment shown below and repeat until you can say the statement with a strong arm.
I want to keep this lack of confidence whilst performing hill starts	On a deeper level, you do not want to learn to drive and will sabotage your own attempts to perform hill starts with confidence. Use the corrective treatment shown below and repeat until you can say the statement with a strong arm	You genuinely want to perform hill starts with confidence and are likely to be successful * Replace with your specific 'problem' area.

As recommended in Chapter Five, 'Your baseline confidence level', in order to stay focused and positive, each morning tap the side of your hand whilst thinking about learning to drive with confidence, and also thinking about your 'problem' areas, such as hill starts. When you have performed this exercise, you should find that your self-confidence increases to such an extent that you are excited about your next lesson and can't wait to practice that hill start because you now have the necessary belief in yourself, and no longer talk to yourself in a negative manner. This is because you are no longer 'Psychologically Reversed' to the belief that you have the skills necessary to perform the task. Now you believe that you can do it, the next step is to reinforce this belief by visualising how you will do it. Exercise One on its own is superb, but the results are amazing when you follow it up with the next exercise.

Some instructors take the view that the best form of teaching is explanation, and that demonstration is only to be used when absolutely necessary or when nothing else has worked. I take the opposite view, and frequently demonstrate manoeuvres etc. to my pupils. My belief is that if you watch something being performed correctly, it is much easier to learn to do it yourself. This exercise is designed to enable you to visualise yourself driving as well as an experienced driver. This technique can be used for general driving, or for specifics such as manoeuvres. You need to pick as your role model someone whom you not only admire but someone who is a competent driver. You may wish to watch your parents, partner or friend, or better still, ask your driving instructor for a demonstration. Your driving instructor is the best person to model yourself on for correct techniques.

For this exercise to be most effective, you not only need to copy the physical actions, but also to think how your role model would think. For example, if you are watching your instructor performing a left turn, the physical aspects that you will notice is that they check their appropriate mirrors, signal, position the car to the left, choose the appropriate gear, and make the turn. In addition, you need to be aware of your instructor's thought processes involved in making the turn. The more realistic you make the visualisation, the more effective and beneficial the exercise.

Exercise Two
'Modelling' your behaviour...

If you have read Chapter Six, 'The basics', you may already be familiar with this exercise.

1. Imagine your chosen role model performing the action that you require help with. Make sure that you remember in detail everything that they do. Run through the memory several times until you can remember it perfectly.

2. Imagine yourself as your role model; sit in the driving seat in the same relaxed posture that your instructor has. See what they would see, and feel the same sense of confidence that they would have.

3. Repeatedly run through this memory in your mind, imagining yourself performing the action in exactly the same way as your instructor. Keep visualising until you can picture yourself performing the action with the same confidence and ability as your instructor.

4. Repeat this exercise as many times as you want, and for as many scenarios as you want, until you can picture yourself performing with as much confidence and competence as your instructor, or chosen role model.

If you have difficulty visualising yourself performing as well as your instructor, you can try the **Basic Tapping Sequence** for 'visualisation for peak performance' from Chapter One, 'How to use this book'.

Chapter Thirteen

Test day stress-busters

If you turned to this page first before reading anything else, then you really are in need of help, and you have come to the right place. Throughout this chapter you will find exercises and techniques that will enable you to perform at your best on your driving test, and to eliminate any negative thoughts of any previous tests that you have failed.

When I was taking my exams at school I remember the feeling of a tightness in my chest, the butterflies in my tummy and the sweaty palms as if it were yesterday. A lucky few will never experience these feelings; I envy those people! However, for the majority of us, the thought of exams of any sort fills us with dread, and if you are in this majority, when in an exam situation I am sure you start to picture all the things that can or will go wrong.

You will find more exercises and techniques in this chapter than in any other chapter, because this is what all your driving lessons, and this whole book is leading up to: getting a test pass. You may find that not all of the exercises are relevant to you, so I suggest that you read through the chapter first and decide which ones you think are suitable for you. I appreciate that there is a lot of information in this chapter, and it's likely that you will want or need to use only some of the exercises. It should take no more than an hour or two to work through the exercises and decide which ones you find the most effective. Ask yourself this: are a couple of hours of your time worth it for the benefit of discovering techniques to help you to pass your test stress-free, with no feelings of nerves or anxiety?

You can perform all of the exercises on your own, and they each only take a few minutes to master. However, it may help to get a sympathetic person to help you with the instructions and to talk you through them. Alternatively, try reading the instructions on to tape and playing them back to yourself if you have difficulty remembering them.

In this chapter you will find all the tools that you need to allow you to banish your nerves, enabling you to feel relaxed and in control, ensuring that you drive as well on your driving test as you would normally do on your driving lesson. What I can't do for you, however, is to improve your drive if you are not yet driving to the required test standard. Therefore, it's imperative that you be guided by your instructor as to when you are ready to take your test. By doing Exercise One, you can determine whether you personally believe that you are physically capable of passing your driving test.

It's only a driving test!

Firstly, I want to look at the worst case scenario: failing a driving test. Perhaps for a few people, a test failure may have serious consequences, e.g. a job riding on the outcome etc., but for the majority of people a test failure results in loss of pride, the cost of taking another test, and a few weeks of having to wait before taking it again. I'm not suggesting that these things aren't important, but it's a relatively small issue. You haven't failed your finals at University and are waiting a year to take them again, your house hasn't burnt down, you haven't lost your job, your best friend hasn't gone off with your partner, you haven't been diagnosed with a serious illness etc. **It's only a driving test!**

If you do fail, don't beat yourself up but say to yourself: 'It's happened, I need to get over it!'

This may sound flippant, but I want you to put taking your driving test into its proper perspective, because in so doing, you won't attach more importance to it than is necessary. If you do feel pressurised into passing, you will benefit reading about 'towards' and 'away' motivation in Chapter Eleven, 'When do you want to pass your driving test?'

If your drive is up to the required standard, and you take on board the advice given throughout this book, there is no reason that you should fail. However, no one, including me, can give a one hundred percent guarantee that you will pass. This may sound very negative, and against the whole thread of the book, but I feel that by reading the above you will put into perspective what failing your driving test actually means to you.

All of the exercises in this chapter will help you to drive to the best of your ability on test day, without the usual nerves and anxiety playing a part. Firstly, try this exercise, which will help you to determine if you really do feel test ready.

Exercise One
Are you ready to take your test?

1. Take a few moments to think about taking your driving test. Imagine that you are sitting in the test centre waiting for the examiner to come out and call your name. Write down the thoughts as soon as they come into your head. This is a useful exercise because it will allow you to get to the bottom of the emotional challenges that you will face on the day.

2. Now you have written down all the emotions that you are feeling, you need to analyse them. This is important, because you need to know whether the emotions that you are feeling are because you are nervous, or because you aren't ready for the test and your emotions are trying to tell you something. If you feel that this is the case, then you need to make sure that you and your instructor genuinely feel that you are physically ready before taking your test. Remember, this chapter is about banishing unnecessary nerves and stress to help you pass your test stress free, not about improving your driving ability.

---

continued...

3. If you can visualise your test in a good light and see yourself passing, then there's nothing to worry about, and you will find that the exercises in this chapter will help you immensely. If, after analysing your emotions, you still have that nagging doubt, then you can be sure that your emotions are trying to tell you something.

Don't let previous failed tests influence your next test

Have you heard the expression: 'be careful what you wish for because it may come true'? Put another way, this translates as 'you get more of what you focus on'. If you have already failed a driving test, it can be difficult to be positive about your next test because you keep running through everything that you previously failed on. This makes it more likely that you will fail again, because the more that you think about what went wrong previously, the more you are telling your unconscious mind that that's what you want to happen again. In effect, you are programming your subconscious mind for failure.

Whilst it's good to learn from previous failed attempts and to take on board the information, thinking about it can often carry a high emotional charge. Therefore, what you need to be able to do is to analyse what went wrong previously in an emotionally detached fashion so you can prevent it from happening again. The exercise that you are going to use now is amazingly effective. It will allow you to think about aspects of previous tests without any emotional baggage, almost as if it had happened to someone else. The benefit of this is two fold: firstly you can analyse the data in a detached fashion, almost as if it had happened to someone else; and secondly, you will be able to take your next test with a clean emotional slate, rather like clearing the inbox on your email. This exercise is also very useful if you are having difficulty with the manoeuvres. If so, you can use it to take away any negative emotions regarding manoeuvres, including frustration that you may feel. Thought Field Therapy is used frequently in the book and to save repetition the procedure is described in detail in Chapter One, 'How to use this book'. Therefore, after reading this section to decide which emotions you wish to deal with, carry out the appropriate techniques as described in Chapter One.

Exercise Two
Eliminate any negative emotions over previous tests and feel positive about your next test

In this exercise, you are going to eradicate any negative emotions attached to any of your previous tests. For it to be most effective, you need to concentrate on the emotions that you feel regarding the failure; they may include anger at yourself for failing, guilt because you let someone down, embarrassment that you had to tell all your friends that you failed, anger or frustration towards yourself or the examiner because you thought it was a bad decision or general stress/anxiety about it. Whatever the emotion it's important that you keep focusing on the feeling whilst carrying out the exercise. Most people will find that the emotion has declined drastically, or even disappeared. If there are still some unpleasant feelings left, you need to keep repeating the exercise until you feel calm, relaxed and detached thinking about the failed test, or whatever you were tuning into.

---

continued...

You can then keep going through this exercise with each negative thought that you have regarding any tests that you have taken. You can also use this exercise if you have had any bad experience whilst learning to drive, or whilst being a passenger in a car. All you need to do is to concentrate on what happened and feel the full emotion of the event, whilst doing the exercise.

In Chapter One, 'How to use this book', you will find the Basic Tapping Sequences along with instructions of how to perform this exercise. Think of which emotions are affecting you most, and use the appropriate sequence for each one.

When you have successfully eradicated all negative thoughts about your previous tests, you can now use Thought Field Therapy to eradicate any nerves or anxiety you feel about your forthcoming test. Just use the appropriate Basic Tapping Sequence relevant to what you are feeling about your test.

In addition to this exercise, also try Exercise Eight, which is based on Neuro Linguistic Programming (NLP). You may choose to use both exercises, or find one is more effective for you than the other: there is no right or wrong exercise to use.

Exercise Three
What low self-esteem?

It may be that as a result of failing previous tests, your self-esteem has taken a battering. It may be because of your lack self-esteem generally, or just with regard to your driving test. Whichever it is, this next exercise will increase your self-esteem, leaving you feeling totally in control and ready to take on the world. If your self-esteem is generally low, it's useful to perform this exercise whilst looking in a mirror and focusing on your lack of self-esteem. If it is directly related to your driving test, instead of looking in a mirror, imagine your feelings of low self-esteem when you are on your driving test.

This is another Thought Field Therapy exercise, so turn to Chapter One, 'How to use this book' and use the **Basic Tapping Sequence** for 'Self-Esteem'.

In the 1970s, Dr. Candace Pert, then a medical student, fell off a horse and was put on morphine. As a scientist, she wondered how the drug worked which, in later years led her to discover what she termed 'molecules of emotion'. Simply put, she discovered that we all have 'docking stations' in our bodies which can receive various chemicals. We may decide to use external or 'exogenous' substances such as drugs which attach themselves to these docking stations to produce a desired emotion. However, what is amazing is that we can produce our very own 'happy chemicals', such as seratonin, or endorphins. The good news is that **every time** that you force yourself to have happy thoughts, this strengthens the neural pathways in the brain that are associated with pleasure, and therefore reinforces the happy chemicals in your body. How often have you heard someone talk about an adrenalin rush, or an endorphin high?

Exercise Four
Choose the emotion that you want to feel for your driving test!

For this exercise to be effective, you need to force yourself to have positive thoughts: this may seem a little odd, and when I tried it for the first time, I gave up after just a few minutes thinking 'what a waste of time, I can't control what I think'. Well now I think, actually, you can.

Whenever you think of your test in a bad light, such as saying to yourself: 'I know that I'm going to fail', force yourself to picture yourself doing well. This will not come naturally to you because from a young age we are bombarded by so many negatives. I'm sure that you'll remember your parents saying things such as: 'don't spill your drink' rather than things such as 'keep your cup upright'. It is easy to talk in negatives rather than positives.

However, like training of any sort, this technique becomes easier the more you try it. Body builders don't go to bed skinny one night and wake up with bulging muscles the next morning; they have to train hard to get their desired physique, and it's the same with your brain. The more that you train your mind to have positive thoughts, the easier it will become. You will find the rest of the exercises in this chapter will help you to achieve positive thoughts.

A good idea is to put sticky notes in prominent places with positive messages about your driving test. Therefore, every time that you see the messages it will encourage you to think positively about your test; and as stated above, the more that you do it, the easier it becomes, and ultimately more effective.

It is interesting how each person defines their emotions. If someone told you that their heart was racing, their breath was caught in their throat, and that their hands were shaking, ask yourself would that be a good or a bad sign if they were just about to go in for their test? Depending on your viewpoint you could say that they were experiencing fear, or alternatively, the wonderful feeling of an adrenalin rush where they were at the height of their performing ability.

Exercise Five
Don't take a driving 'test' or 'exam'

This next exercise may sound somewhat childish, but it's very effective. Every time that you think of the word 'test' or 'exam' try to find another word or phrase to substitute it with which makes your subconscious mind believe that it is a more pleasurable experience. For example, if at work or college you have to do a 'project', this usually conjures up visions of hard work, long hours, and not much fun. How about if you substituted the word 'project' for the word 'adventure', ask yourself how much more fun would it seem now?

How about if you thought of your driving test as an 'opportunity' to show off your skills? All of a sudden, the 'test' doesn't seem as bad, does it? I suggest you play around with this idea and be as inventive as possible; the sillier the better, because in so doing, every time that you do this, you are lessening the scary thought of the word 'test' or 'exam'. I'd be interested to know what replacements readers come up with for these two words; why not put in on the blog at www.Lofaway2pass.com

Exercise Six
The happiness and relaxation trigger

You can use this exercise and exercise seven for any situation, but I suggest you use it here to help you to remain calm and relaxed about your forthcoming driving test. Close your eyes and remember a time when you felt wonderfully happy and excited. See what you saw, feel what you felt, and hear what you heard. Look at the picture of this memory in your mind and notice:

1. It is a still photograph or a movie? If it is a still photograph see if you can change it to a movie.

2. Is it in colour or black and white? If it is in black and white see if you can change it to colour and make the colours as bright and bold as possible. Make the picture as big and vivid as you can.

3. Can you smell anything? Try to remember any smells that were associated with this memory.

4. If there are any sounds such as music, listen to them and let them wash over you again, stimulating the memory.

5. Let the strong feelings you had flow through you and see if you can intensify them.

6. When the feelings are as wonderful as you can possibly recall them, press together your thumb and your middle finger to anchor this feeling. Do this several times when you are feeling most happy in your memory.

7. As you continue to look at the picture/movie, float into it so that you are a part of it—look around you and make it even more vivid. Anchor this feeling again.

Exercise Seven
The success trigger

For this exercise close your eyes and remember a time when you did something brilliantly. It doesn't matter what the something was—it could be knitting, bricklaying, nuclear physics or history. The important thing is that mastering this skill/subject made you feel happy and successful.

Recall the satisfaction you felt when you were going through this process successfully—each step taking you nearer to achieving your goal. See what you saw, feel what you felt, and hear what you heard. Look at the picture of this memory in your mind and notice the way that it makes you feel.

Repeat steps 1-7 of your happiness trigger. Before your instructor collects you for your driving test, take some time in a quiet place to:

1. Visualise your happy self and step into it.

2. Visualise your successful self and step into it.

3. Power up your positive memories by using your anchors.

You can use your anchor (pressing your thumb and finger together) anytime to feel immediately relaxed, happy and ready to succeed.

Exercise Eight
How to change a bad feeling into a really good one

This technique can be used as well as Exercise Two to eliminate anxiety or nerves. Feel free to use them both, or whichever one you prefer.

1. Close your eyes and concentrate on the bad feeling, whether it be nerves or anxiety, and let it wash through you.

2. Notice where the feeling is and it what direction it is moving.

3. Visualise yourself pulling this feeling outside of your body and make the actions with your hand.

4. Allow the feeling to move in its original direction for a moment.

5. Take hold of the feeling and start to turn it in the opposite direction, using your hand and make the movements.

6. Spin the feeling faster and faster in the opposite direction to the one it was moving in—notice as you spin it faster and faster that the feeling changes from a bad one to a good one.

7. Keep spinning the feeling until you achieve an overwhelming feeling of happiness and calm.

8. Imagine the feeling is saturated in your favourite colour.

continued...

9. Push the still spinning feeling back inside your body and let it carry on spinning from the tips of your toes to the top of your head, releasing waves of colour.

10. When this wonderful feeling reaches its height—let it explode out of the top of your head.

11. Notice how incredibly relaxed and peaceful you feel, and ready to take on anything.

Exercise Nine
Using Timelines to program yourself for success

Timelines are a form of Neuro Linguistic Programming exercise that can be used to remove negative feelings from the past and to program positive feelings into the future. Try this exercise to set your future goal of passing your driving test:

1. Visualise your life as a line stretching into your past, through your present and into your future as a straight Timeline. Your past will usually be behind you and the present will usually pass through you, with your future being in front of you. For some people, the Timeline may pass from left to right or vice versa.

2. Relax and imagine your Timeline stretching out into the future (you need to set the actual amount of time, e.g. three months, six months etc., whatever is realistic for you), to a time when you have passed your driving test.

3. Notice where that position is in front of you.

4. Point to that point—the point where you have passed your test.

continued...

5. Visualise a picture of yourself, when you have passed your driving test and feel what you will feel, see what you will see, and hear what you will hear when you visualise that picture.

6. Increase these feelings and the brightness of the image until you really want and desire it.

7. Take that image and move it over your Timeline and place it past a point slightly further than you imagine it will be in the future. Next, move it closer to a place where it feels just right and you are certain it will happen. Bring back all of the feelings, sounds and pictures you saw in step 5, then anchor this feeling by pressing together your thumb and forefinger.

8. Take this image out further in to the future, place yourself on this point on the Timeline and look back from the future along the Timeline to the present. Look at all the positive benefits you have achieved by passing your driving test and what they have meant to you. Anchor these feelings as above.

9. Bring the image back to now (the present) and anchor the positive feelings again. Then take the image in to the past and experience the thing that you have achieved as a past event. It is now something that you have already done.

10. Bring the image up to the present and into now. Then let it move to a place that feels and looks right. Ask yourself where this image has settled. Look at that point and visualise again the amazing feelings of successfully achieving this goal. Is it already possible or definite in the near future?

Exercise Ten
Timeline Two

1. Stand on your present on your Timeline then slowly walk forward to the point where you have passed your driving test. You are now in the future.

2. Turn around and look back through the lessons and steps that successfully enabled you to achieve this.

3. Slowly walk back through the steps, visualising, feeling and seeing them one by one and feeling the feelings of achievement at each stage. Anchor them one by one.

4. When you get back to the present look forward again to the future successful you and bring back the image, knowing that you have achieved all of the steps you need to meet this reality, in your future.

Exercise Eleven
Driving into the future

By using the above Timeline exercises, picture a Timeline some way into the future, whether it be a couple of hours or several weeks after your test. Decide on a destination that you would like to go to; perhaps your friend's house, or the beach, and drive there in your mind. Enjoy the journey and feel the same sense of achievement and confidence that you will have as if you have already passed your driving test.

A final thought

By now you should have an armoury of techniques to take you into combat! Just remember, if you can drive to test standard whilst with your instructor, then there is no reason why you can't do the same on your driving test. I think it's important to reiterate the point I made at the start of this chapter; this chapter is not intended to improve your driving ability but it is intended to eliminate any negative thoughts that are preventing you from performing to the best of your ability on your driving test, and to give you the resources to picture yourself passing.

Remember, your instructor is the best judge of when you are ready for your driving test. If you think that you are ready, but your instructor keeps putting you off, this is due to one of two reasons. The most likely is that your instructor genuinely doesn't feel that you are ready, and doesn't want you to waste your money and have the disappointment of failure. The second, and thankfully, very unlikely reason is that the instructor can make a bit more money from you before putting you in for your test. Be rest assured though, this is not at all common as speaking as an instructor myself, our reputation is important to us, and you don't often come across an unscrupulous instructor. Therefore, be rest assured, your instructor has your best interests at heart, and if he doesn't put you in for your test, there will be a good reason for this.

A good idea to help you get some confidence for your driving test is to do a 'mock test' with your driving instructor. Use the techniques in this chapter to prepare you. You will find a mock test of most benefit to you if you treat it as if it were the real thing, rather than with the attitude of 'Oh well, it doesn't matter, it's only pretend'. I guarantee, if you don't perform well on your mock test, don't expect to perform better on the genuine one. Your instructor will probably suggest a mock test as a matter of course, but if they don't, make sure that you suggest it and do one in plenty of time, so that should you not be up to the standard, you can re-arrange your test date to give you time for more lessons.

It's not a good idea to do a mock test on a Monday, if your test is on Wednesday, as it would be very demoralising to fail. You need to allow enough time so that should you not be up to the required test standard, then you can postpone your actual driving test with no loss of fee; this is currently three working days, so if your test is on a Friday, you will need to cancel the preceding Monday. However, please check this information with your instructor as this may change.

I hope that you find these techniques useful, and it just remains for me to say:

Good luck!

Chapter Fourteen

**The top ten reasons for failure
and how to avoid them**

The current overall pass rate
is just forty-two percent
and the first time pass rate is even lower

Why is the failure rate so high? Driving Standards Agency
has published a list of the top ten reasons for failure, and
not surprisingly, every manoeuvre features on this list.
However, the majority of test candidates who fail do so
because of a lack of planning and judgement. You may be
physically able to drive to a high standard, but this is not
enough to ensure a test pass.

As well as being able to drive, you have to have an
awareness of what's happening around you, and to act
accordingly. However, this is where the problems arise
during the test, because nerves can play such a large part
on how you are able to perform on the day. So many people
say after their test: 'but I **never** do that normally!'

A recent survey* showed that over half of the people
questioned thought that they would fail their test because
of 'doing something silly' on the day that they wouldn't
normally do on a driving lesson. Furthermore, ninety
percent of the people surveyed believed that their negative
thoughts and resulting nerves would have an impact on
their test result.

In the same survey, ninety-five percent of the people
questioned said it would be wonderful if they could go for
their test feeling: 'excited because I have absolute belief
and confidence in my ability to pass'. My belief is that
now you have worked through the various exercises and
techniques in this book, you can have this feeling, and if
you go for your test feeling this confident in your ability,
then you will have the best chance possible of passing your
test on the first attempt.

Although your instructor will teach you the physical driving skills to enable you to pass your test, the standard method of learning to drive does little to increase your confidence in your own ability, reduce your nerves on the day, and therefore mentally prepare you for your test; that is why the exercises in this book are so useful.

Here are the Top Ten reasons for failure according to DSA. Take a few minutes to look through the list and note which ones you identify with. You may find it helpful to think back to your driving lessons and ask yourself which driving skills your instructor needs to keep practicing with you. When you have done this, you will have an accurate idea as to where your strengths and weaknesses lie and, if you haven't done so already, you can then use the relevant exercises and techniques in the book to help you.

- **Observation at junctions -** ineffective observation and judgement
- **Reverse parking -** ineffective observation or lack of accuracy
- **Use of mirrors -** not checking or not acting on the information
- **Moving away -** ineffective observation or control when moving away
- **Use of signals -** not given, not cancelled or misleading signals
- **Incorrect positioning -** at roundabouts, lanes and bends
- **Reversing around a corner -** ineffective observation or lack of accuracy
- **Lack of steering control -** steering too early or leaving it too late
- **Turn round in road -** ineffective observation or lack of accuracy
- **Inappropriate speed -** travelling too slowly

The Madness of manoeuvres

Every single manoeuvre features in the top ten reasons for failure as published by Driving Standards Agency

If you can perform all the manoeuvres accurately, with good observation and control, with no input from your instructor, then skip this section. If however, you feel that you need help to master the manoeuvres, then read on. As you may have read in Chapter Seven, 'Master the manoeuvres', getting a manoeuvre right nine times out of ten is really good but not good enough if the one you get wrong is the one you do on your driving test.

I have spoken to some examiners who really try not to fail pupils on just manoeuvres, but they have a job to do, and if the manoeuvre is not up to the required standard then just a single mistake such as missing a look out of the back window or lack of accuracy is enough to result in test failure.

Can you afford to pay for a retest, not to mention the upset of failure just because you clipped a kerb?

Even though manoeuvres only account for a few minutes of your test, it's vitally important that you are comfortable and confident in your ability to get them right. That's why if there is any doubt in your mind about your ability to perform the manoeuvres to the required standard, make sure you complete the exercises in Chapter Seven, 'Mastering the manoeuvres'. The techniques you will learn will ensure that you are fully prepared. Remember, **every single manoeuvre** features in the top ten reasons for failure, so don't let them be your downfall.

Mirror, mirror on the wall...

As you look through the list, you will see that the reasons for failure fall into two basic categories: observation and judgement, and physical ability. Ask yourself how difficult it is to look in your mirrors whilst driving. When you go on your driving test, does a neck brace mysteriously appear around your neck as the examiner gets into the car, which prevents your head from moving, or do your eyes suddenly start to hurt as soon as you look in the mirror, or perhaps your elaborate hairstyle prevents you from turning around to check your blind spot? Of course not, but look again at the list of reasons for failure:

Six out of ten of them are attributable to lack of use of mirrors and observation

So why do so many people fail their test for these reasons? If it were so easy to make sure that you use your mirrors effectively, act on what you see, check your blind spots when necessary and keep good all round observation, then the pass rate would be much higher. At least, that is the theory.

How many people do you know who have failed their test because of lack of use of mirrors or observation? Perhaps you have even done so yourself. However, why do people fail their driving test because of a failure to do correctly something so obvious and easy to learn? It is because when you are feeling nervous you forget the most basic skills. I have thought about this issue a lot and I have a theory why people miss basic mirror checks on their test and that theory is that people learn from their mistakes. If you lift your foot off the clutch too quickly, the car stalls, so you learn to take your foot off more slowly. If you try to go up a hill in a high gear, the car struggles, so you learn that you need a lower gear going up hill.

These two errors have a tangible, physical consequence. Therefore, you learn from your mistake.

However, a missed mirror check during a lesson or test may have no physical consequence, but when it does, the physical consequences can be fatal: swapping lanes in front of another car, or braking harshly so that the car behind runs into you, or not checking a blind spot and knocking a child off their bike. However, these events are highly unlikely to occur during a lesson or test as your instructor (or accompanying driver) will prevent them from happening, as they will be more aware and experienced than you about what is happening around the car. You may never get the opportunity to learn from such mistakes until you've passed your test because it would obviously put people's lives at risk (and let's hope that you never do get that opportunity). There can be no controlled errors where mirror checks and observation are concerned.

> **'I always know what's happening around me,**
> **check my mirrors, and act on what I see.'**

If you can say the above with total conviction, then you do not need to read this section. However, if your instructor has to keep reminding you to check your mirrors and blind spots, then read on. It's very simple; all you have to do is:

Look in the appropriate mirrors before
Signalling
Changing Speed
Changing Direction

As we have already said if it were that simple then no one would fail their test due to observation errors and missed mirror checks, or acting inappropriately on observations made. In the survey mentioned earlier, seventy percent of the people questioned said that their instructor has to prompt them on a regular basis. It is hard to understand why pupils need reminding to check their mirrors, knowing that they are aware that there can be fatal consequences of not doing this.

'I'm sorry that your child is dead, but I just forgot to check my blind spot.'

I'm using shock tactics but I think they are necessary as death is the potential consequence **every single time** a driver forgets to check their mirrors or blind spot. If the police visited your house to advise that a close relative had been murdered, perhaps shot or stabbed, how would you feel towards the murderer? Imagine instead that this relative had been killed by a driver swapping lanes in front of them. How would you feel towards the driver of that car? Would you feel the same as you would feel towards the murderer? Even though the intention is completely different, the outcome is still the same. The scenarios described above should be enough to ensure that you are **always** aware of what's happening around you, and that you take full responsibility for your actions.

Getting the right perspective

When I was learning to drive, I was a student and my fellow students and I would often discuss how well our driving lessons had gone. The question most often heard was: 'So, how many times did you stall?' When I talk to my pupils now, they still ask the same question of their friends. I don't remember ever saying: 'It was brilliant, although I stalled ten times, I never missed a mirror check!' People don't seem to consider errors made in checking their mirrors as important or worthy of comment as they do errors made stalling their car. This is incredible. If you are more concerned about how many times you stalled, rather than your mirrors and awareness, then I think that you need a lesson in perspective.

If you miss a mirror check, you can potentially kill someone; however, the usual consequences of stalling are that you will hold a few people up for a few seconds.

I'm not suggesting that stalling is a good thing to do; I am saying that if you are more concerned with stalling the car than with your mirror checks then you need to get things into perspective. Stalling may have serious consequences, especially if you stall in the middle of a roundabout, or at traffic lights just as they are about to change, but I don't understand why people place much more emphasis on this than missing a mirror check. Ask yourself how many times you keep thinking about the few times that you stalled on your lesson, compared to the many times that you missed a mirror or blind spot check. Pupils often get very nervous and panic when they have stalled because they feel embarrassed and are worried about what the other drivers around them are thinking, or that they are holding people up, and annoying other drivers. They aren't unduly concerned when they have missed a mirror check and they should be.

Promise yourself that from this moment on you will never again miss a mirror check and will always be aware of what's happening around you.

I hope that this section will have shown you the importance of mirrors, blind spots and observation, but I suggest you work through Chapter Six, 'The basics' to ensure that this is firmly entrenched in your mind for good.

**Remember, a car is a potentially a lethal weapon and you are in control of it.
It takes less than a second to check your mirrors, but if you don't, you will regret it for the rest of your life if you cause a fatal accident.**

Don't fail the physical!

If you refer back to the top ten reasons for failure, surprisingly the physical skill of driving doesn't feature very highly. Only 'moving away under control' and 'lack of steering control' find their way into the top ten.

You have probably realised by now that the physical ability to drive is the easiest bit to master, and that the hardest part is the thinking behind it. However, what can you do if on your test, the nerves get the better of you, and the physical ability to drive seems to leave you temporarily? So many people drive really well during their lessons, and then go to pieces on their test. What maybe of little consequence on your lesson can turn into a catastrophe if you let it get to you on your test.

If you usually drive well on your lesson, then remember, you can also do it on your test as well; you just may not think that you can!

As you learned earlier, no good instructor will let a pupil take their test before they are ready, as it's very demoralising to fail your test. Your instructor wants you to be as prepared as possible, so you don't have to go through the upset of failing. Therefore, it's in everyone's interest to make sure you are fully prepared.

Only clutch and steering control feature in this section, and if you have difficulty in these areas, please don't put in for your test until you feel totally confident in your ability. When you have to do an uphill start, if you are scared that you may roll back and feeling nervous about it, then trust me, you are not ready for your test.

So, ask yourself (and your instructor) if your physical driving ability is up to test standard. If it isn't, carry on working on it until it is; but if it is, and you are concerned that nerves will get to you on your test and prevent you from driving as well as you normally would, then make sure you work through Chapter Thirteen, 'Test day stress-busters'. You will find that so long as your drive is up to the required standard, then you will not suddenly lose your ability to drive due to nerves.

Perfect planning and execution

I suggest that you now look again at the top ten reasons for failure. Which ones do you think are related to planning and decision-making? I think that the following reasons for failure could be prevented, or at least reduced with more thought:

Observation at junctions
Incorrect positioning
Inappropriate speed
Use of signals

How many times have you said 'If only...' followed by a range of comments, such as, 'I'd seen that car at the roundabout', 'remembered to turn my signal on/off', 'stayed in the correct lane', 'spotted the speed limit sign' etc.?

After the event, it's very easy to be full of remorse, bitterness, anger and a range of other emotions, but that just makes you feel worse about failing your test. How much better would it be to say: 'I drove to the best of my ability, and was really in the "zone" and was aware of everything happening around me.'? If your physical drive is up to the required standard, then how frustrating would it be to fail on something as simple as missing a speed limit, or forgetting to cancel your signal?

Prior planning prevents poor performance

Remembering this statement is all very well when preparing for an examination; all you have to do is know what's on the syllabus and revise accordingly. However, when talking about driving, we are talking about making instant judgements and decisions that can affect lives; a split second decision that could result in life or death. Perhaps this sounds a bit heavy. But consider this: so is a car when it hits you at 70mph. Therefore, it's imperative that your judgement is sound and that you always drive with utmost concentration and thought. This is perhaps the hardest part of all when learning to drive.

Awareness and planning

I once taught a pupil who was meant to be taking her test in two weeks. We were on a wide, straight country lane, doing about fifty mph with several cars approaching from the opposite direction. Up ahead there was a tractor travelling at about ten mph, and we were rapidly getting closer and closer to it. My pupil asked: 'Shall I slow down?' This particular pupil frequently didn't judge situations very well and tended to rely on me for everything. I had been trying to get her to think for herself a little more. Therefore, instead of telling her to slow down, I said: 'no, that's fine, keep at fifty mph', to which my pupil replied, 'but if I do, I'll hit it!'. To this my reply was: 'Well, stop asking silly questions then!'

Firstly, let's look at the easy part; increased awareness and planning. The items that are on the top ten reasons for failure, such as making sure you are in the correct lane on a roundabout, using your signals correctly and cancelling them, making sure you notice all the changes in speed limits and other appropriate road signs are easily dealt with.

Your instructor will teach you all of the above, but remembering them during your test is a different matter. Often it's not lack of ability, but lack of memory that causes the problems. For example, how many times do you forget which lane you should be in on a roundabout, forget to change to second gear for a junction, or forget to cancel your signal?

On countless occasions I've been with a pupil who is ranting on about other drivers who don't give a signal, saying: 'If he'd indicated off the roundabout, I could have gone, but I didn't know which way he was going'. I then have to remind them to put their own signal on because they have forgotten it. The many visualisation techniques in the book will help you, and you will find that your awareness and planning skills will increase, and the number of times that you instructor has to repeat things such as: 'don't forget to cancel your signal', will decrease rapidly, the result of which will be that you should be able to take your driving test in fewer lessons than if you hadn't used the techniques.

Judgement

This is the difficult area for many people because a lot of judgement is about common sense, and it is very hard to teach common sense. On many occasions, I've had a pupil ask the question: 'Can I go?', whilst we are waiting at a junction and there is a large truck coming towards us. I feel that some pupils do have a death wish. Many people also have a problem with spatial awareness. They may try to fit through a gap that a motorcycle wouldn't attempt, or wait when there's a gap that a bus could get through.

One of the best methods that I've found for improving judgement is to get pupils to watch other people driving and making a decision whether to pull out of a junction or roundabout or not, and asking the pupils to decide if they would think it was safe to pull out. A good exercise to try when you are a passenger is to imagine that you are driving and see if the driver makes the same decision to wait or go as you would have done if you were driving. You may be very surprised.

Often, when you watch a good driver, they will go for a seemingly impossible gap on a roundabout that you wouldn't even consider. You must remember that they have experience behind them, and are very competent at clutch control. An experienced driver will have pulled out whilst you would be still trying to decide whether your clutch is at bite or not.

'Can I go?'

The problem with this question is that if you had pulled out instead of asking whether you should pull out or not, then you probably could have made the move, but by the time you have asked the question, it's too late. You can see now the problems associated with judgement; it's often a split second decision. Unlike a manoeuvre when you can take time to do it properly and your instructor can talk you through it stage by stage, judgement is instant.

Therefore, although judgement can be taught to a certain degree, for example, if you could walk across a road as a pedestrian, then you have time to go in the car, it's ultimately a matter of experience. As one of the main objectives of this book is to reduce the number of lessons that you will need, what I am now saying seems to go against what we are trying to achieve; on the one hand I'm trying to reduce the number of lessons you will require, and on the other, I'm telling you that you need more experience. How can you do both?

As you have learned from previous chapters, you need to watch other people drive, and in turn, learn from their knowledge and expertise, and transfer this to your own driving. If you have one lesson per week, you aren't going to gain experience and judgment very quickly, but by utilising the visualisation exercises, you will be re-running through your lessons, and can look back at what you would have done differently if you were able to go back to the same situation again.

When can I take my test?

Many people complain about the long time that they have to wait before they can take their driving test. As over half of the tests conducted in this country result in failure, then theoretically these waiting times could be halved if candidates were at the required standard before taking their test. This is one of the reasons for DSA publishing the top ten reasons for failure, and consequently for me writing this chapter. You will know yourself when you feel confident in your ability, but your instructor will advise you when he feels that you are at the required standard.

If you are in any doubt, then look no further than the advice from DSA: 'If you're not getting it right all of the time without your instructor's help, then you're not ready to take your test'. Just think back to your last lesson; how often did your instructor have to help or remind you about something? To be ready for your test, you need to be able to drive for the whole lesson with no help or advice from your instructor other than your instructor giving you directions. If this sounds harsh, please remember; when you have passed your test, your instructor is not there to help you on that steep hill when you stall, or to tell you if it's okay to go at that busy roundabout.

Chapter Fifteen

You've passed your test - now what?

Passing your driving test is the best feeling in the world. You will feel a sense of achievement, freedom, excitement and a range of other wonderful emotions. Unless you do something very silly and get points on your licence, **nobody can take your licence away from you.** You have earned it, but it's up to you to keep it.

'I've passed my test and I'm going for a drive - now!'

If you have your own car, then you can drive it immediately after you have passed your test. For some people that is a fantastic feeling and they can't wait to get behind the wheel. For some, however, this is a very scary prospect and the thought of driving on their own for the first time fills them with dread. Both of these feeling are perfectly natural; this leads us back to this confidence and competence issue, and of course, the best new drivers are the ones with equal amounts of both. To be able to pass your test, you obviously have to be competent, so let's now consider two drivers of the same ability, but one over confident and the other lacking in confidence. The first driver can't wait to get behind the wheel; perhaps picking their friends up to show off their car which now has a distinct lack of 'L' plates. They go for a drive, without a care in the world thinking that they are as good as anyone else on the road: 'Well, I've passed my test, haven't I?' Now, let's consider the driver who has just passed, and feels really scared about going out for the first time, and decides to have a little drive on their own on a quiet estate to get used to the car.

The first driver could potentially be a danger to themselves and other road users because they are so over confident that they have forgotten that for the last few months or so they have had the back up of their instructor should they make a mistake. Ultimately, it's now solely up to them to make decisions. However, the driver who is lacking in confidence can also be a danger because they are likely to be very hesitant in their driving.

As you learned at the very start of the book, I consider a good driver to be one who has equal amounts of confidence and competence, and if you have worked through the exercises relevant to you throughout the book, you should feel confident in your ability, but aware that you still have a lot to learn. If you are full of confidence, remember, it's **very, very different** driving on your own without the support of your instructor. You have passed your test, but now is the time that you are going to gain valuable experience. I would suggest that for a little while you build your competence up in areas that you are familiar with. The hour after you've passed your test, you should perhaps refrain from deciding to go to London on the motorway, or drive through the centre of a large city that you are not familiar with. Conversely, if you still feel really nervous about driving on your own, remember that the examiner had faith in your ability, otherwise they wouldn't have issued you with a pass certificate. Therefore, be cautious and at first drive around areas that you are familiar with, and as a result you will begin to have more confidence in your ability.

'I may have passed, but it will be ages before I get to drive.'

If you don't have access to a car straight away after passing your test, you can feel that passing your driving test is a bit of a let down. However, take heart from the fact that you've done it, and you don't have to do it again. Quite often I get calls from people who have passed their test a long time ago, but have only just decided to take up driving. As you learned earlier on in the book, the mind works by repetition and if you don't do something for a while, it's very easy to forget. Think back to the last exam that you took. If you had to re sit it now, how much of it do you think that you would remember? Therefore, if having passed your test you don't intend to drive for a while, I think that it's a sensible idea to have a couple of refresher lessons before getting behind the wheel again. You will be surprised how quickly you remember everything that you have been taught.

Safe driving for life

Ultimately, this is what you are aiming to achieve after having passed your driving test. The test itself is only the first step before hopefully many years of enjoyable safe driving. When I first passed my test I had a huge row with my Mum. As a very confident seventeen year old, I believed that as I had passed my test, there was nothing else to learn. I was driving, with my Mum as a passenger, and I recall trying to go through a gap between two parked cars that was too tight. Mum told me not to go and I'm embarrassed to say now that I said to her: 'You can't tell me what to do, I've passed my test'. I truthfully thought that because I was now a qualified driver, I was immune to making any mistakes. It's not until I look back to that incident that I realise how naïve I was. As a new driver, remember that you are just starting out and you are bound to make mistakes; no one is perfect. However, what you must be aware of is that mistakes made whilst driving are potentially fatal. Therefore, enjoy your driving, but take note of the fact that there will always be something new to learn.

The Pass Plus Scheme

The Pass Plus is very well worth doing as not only does it give you valuable post driving test experience, but it will also save you about thirty percent on your car insurance as it gives you a one year no claims bonus with some insurers. For example, if your insurance premium would be £1000, it would be £300 cheaper with the Pass Plus. There is no test at the end of the course, but your instructor will assess you on your ability to drive in the town and countryside, at night and in adverse weather, and on dual carriageways and motorways. With the exception of motorway driving, you may already have experience in these other areas, but the Pass Plus scheme will increase your skills in these areas. The Pass Plus is not compulsory, but I do feel that it is very beneficial to all newly qualified drivers.

The 'P' plates debate

The introduction of 'P' plates is theoretically a great idea. Other drivers would see that a driver has only recently passed their test and therefore would show much more consideration, stay further back so as not to 'crowd' the new driver, and give them a bit more leeway if for example they took a little longer than normal to emerge from a junction. However, in my experience, this is often not how it works in practice. There are a great number of drivers who are thoughtful and considerate, and who, if they see 'P' plates will think: 'Oh, poor thing, I bet they feel really nervous having to start off on this big hill, I'll stay well back to give them loads of room, so they don't have to worry about me being too close'. However, for every driver who thinks along these lines, there are a great many more people who have been driving for years and unfortunately, their opinion tends to be along the lines of: 'Well, they've passed their test, haven't they? If they can't drive then they shouldn't be on the road'.

Ultimately, the choice is yours whether to use 'P' plates or not. Depending on the situation, you may find that some drivers are more accommodating, whereas others may tend to be more intimidatory. My suggestion is if it makes you feel better having them on to make other drivers aware that you are new to driving, try them and judge the response for yourself.

Road rage

A phrase that is often used is: 'treat others how you would like to be treated yourself' and there isn't a more appropriate phrase to sum up driving with consideration for other road users. We all know that road rage is on the increase. We live in a society that is increasingly lacking in tolerance and the slightest error can bring out the worst in people, and even I have felt frustration at other people not driving properly. I think that it's appropriate to remind anyone reading this book that no one is perfect and this includes driving. Therefore, before you get angry with another driver, consider how many times you've made a similar mistake.

If you do tend to get angry easily, then you can use the **Basic Tapping Sequence** for anger that you will find in Chapter One, 'How to use this book'. Getting angry is a natural response when another driver has made an error in judgement, but remember that when you get angry, your own judgement is clouded and you are more likely to make an error yourself.

'Ringing' and 'drinking'

What I am going to share with you now is common sense, but as you read earlier, not everyone always has this trait. We all know the possible consequences of drinking and driving, using a mobile phone whilst driving etc., but even though everyone knows that doing these things is wrong, they so often blatantly ignore the law. What is of most concern is that drivers are more worried about 'getting caught' than they are of the possible consequences of carrying out these actions. If you read Chapter Fourteen, 'The top ten reasons for failure and how to avoid them', you will be aware of the consequences of missed mirror checks, and drinking and driving, or using a mobile phone carry the same possibly fatal consequences. Forget the fact that you may get caught, instead just ask yourself, how would you ever live with yourself if you caused a fatal accident because you were on your mobile phone, or changing a CD, or because your reactions were impaired after having a drink?

A final thought

Many of my pupils have suggested that I have a section for their thoughts and comments about learning to drive, and here is a selection of them.

Just because you can drive, it doesn't mean that you are ready for your test—it's everything else that goes with it.
Becky O'Donoghue

If you don't do your mirror checks when you are on a driving lesson with your instructor, what makes you think you are going to do them on your own after you have passed your test?
Carol Hill

The car is a machine not a toy!
Lisa-Marie Graham

Coasting feels really scary because it's just like skating on ice!
Lisa-Marie Graham

I think that women make better drivers and have less accidents as they are always looking around because they are nosey!
Lisa-Marie Graham

You may feel frustrated when learning to drive, but imagine how your poor instructor feels!
Sophie Burgess

As soon as I got home from my lesson, I sat on the sofa with a dinner plate for a steering wheel and practiced my manoeuvres!
Razia Bi

I can't imagine myself driving without my instructor being there.
Iram Jhangir

My drive really started to improve when I realised that the responsibility stops with me, not my instructor.
Anon.

You really need to do every mirror check as you don't know which is the one that is going to save your life.
Anon.

There's no need to panic, after all, it's just a man with a clipboard!
Kayleigh Mueller

Just because you can stop quickly, such as if the traffic lights change, doesn't mean that the driver behind can. That's why you want to know what's behind you all the time so you can plan well ahead.
Insa Hussain

I thought my driving test would be like stage fright; once you got out there it would get better, but it didn't, it just

got worse. After the Thought Field Therapy, I then tried to get nervous about my forthcoming test, but I couldn't even think of it, my mind went totally blank.
Alex Radcliffe

I had three driving instructors previously, and I really thought that I wasn't born with the 'driving gene'! I have now passed my test on the first attempt and feel so proud of myself.
Anon.

'If you doubt your power to achieve, you add power to your doubts.'

anon.

Well, that's it! You've reached the end of the book, and hopefully you have now passed your test stress-free and in fewer lessons with the help of your instructor and this book. It just remains for me to say, enjoy your driving, drive with consideration to other road users, and please add your comments to the blog at www.Lofaway2pass. com. You never know, your comment may be the one that inspires another learner.

If you want to find out how this system has helped other learners, take a look at the comments at
www.tapstherapy.co.uk.
If you wish to have your own comments added, please contact me at tapstherapy@aol.com

Further reading and useful contacts

Website for the book:
www.Lofaway2pass.com

Author's other websites:
www.tapstherapy.co.uk www.fastpass.vpweb.co.uk

Sandra Read's website:
www.freedomfromdyslexia.co.uk

Sean Quigley's website:
www.tft-vt.com

To order more copies of the book, contact the website for the book or:
www.authorhouse.co.uk/bookstore

For everything you need to know about learning to drive and passing your driving test:
www.2pass.co.uk

To contact Dr. Roger Callahan, founder of Thought Field Therapy:
www.tftrx.com roger@tftrx.com

Thought Field Therapy organisations, or to find a therapist in your area:
www.atft.com www.btfta.co.uk

Website design - Steve Light
www.breadandbuddha.co.uk

Janet Thomson
www.powertochange.me.uk

Rebecca Collins (Freelance Editor)
rebecca.collins@daftcat.co.uk

For queries about Special Arrangements for Driving Tests contact:

www.driving-tests.co.uk
Information on Learning Styles available from:
The British Dyslexia Association
Tel: 0118 966 8271
www.bdadyslexia.org.uk

Daisy Books – digital talking books
Daisy Books and information on alternative formats are available from:
www.YourDolphin.com

Information on Memory Strategies and Mindmapping
www.buzanworld.com

Information on Dyspraxia available from:
Adult Dyspraxia Helpline: 020 7435 5443
Dyspraxia Foundation, 8 West Alley, Hitchin, Herts SG5 1EG
Tel: 01462 454986 (Helpline)
Tel: 01462 455016 (Admin)
www.dyspraxiafoundation.org.uk

Ott, P., *How to Detect and Manage Dyslexia* (1997; Heinemann, Oxford).

Krupska & Klein *Demystifying Dyslexia* (1995; London Language and Literacy Unit).

Brain Gym
www.braingym.org.uk

AbilityNet – offers free advice and information about technology that can assist people with many difficulties/ disabilities.
www.abilitynet.org.uk

Texthelp Read and Write - a program designed for Dyslexic learners which enables text to be read from any windows program.
www.texthelp.com

Eye Level Reading Rulers and Coloured Overlays
www.crossboweducation.com

Information on Specialist Dyslexia Teachers and Dyslexia Assessments
www.patoss-dyslexia.org

Music and Learning
www.mozarteffect.com

Books and Contacts for NLP
Introducing NLP
Joseph O'Connor & John Seymour

An Insider's Guide to Submodalities
Richard Bandler and Will MacDonald

Frogs Into Princes
Bandler and Grinder

Magic In Action
Richard Bandler

Using Your Brain for a Change
Richard Bandler

Paul McKenna Training
www.paulmckenna.com

The Society of NLP
www.purenlp.com

Printed in the United Kingdom by
Lightning Source UK Ltd., Milton Keynes
138139UK00002B/3/P